A Tale of
Two Railways

A Tale of
Two Railways

My career driving trains in England and Denmark

ALAN EVANS

THE CHOIR PRESS

First published in the United Kingdom in 2025 by
The Choir Press

ISBN 978-1-78963-518-8

To Susanne
My ever-tolerant wife

Contents

Foreword

During my career covering forty-eight years, I have had several roles within the railway industry, both in England and Denmark.

This book tells how I came to work for the railways and details my working life in both countries, drawing parallels between two state-owned organisations.

Formative Years

I was born in 1954 in West Sussex and as far back as I can remember have been interested in transport. Living in a small village, the vehicles of Southdown Motor Services were of great interest as they were our means of getting about, the family not owning a car. We had an hourly service between Midhurst and Brighton, route 22, and with the many connections available we were able to reach Worthing, Horsham, Bognor Regis and Chichester quite easily. It was all double-deck operation at that time and wherever possible the top deck was used, giving fantastic views of the Sussex countryside.

My grandmother lived in Southsea and when visiting her we took the train from Pulborough. At that time, the fast Portsmouth services were in the hands of 4COR units, and the stopping services were 2BIL/2HAL units. A vivid memory is of the vast gap, for me, between the train and platform at Fratton and the noisy DEMU sets on the Southampton services. Little did I know that I would come to work on such diesel units later on! Southsea was always fascinating because of the Corporation buses in their maroon and white livery, and of course there were also the trolleybuses. My father always took me for a ride on one to the harbour, circular route 17/18, and I always managed to choose the long way round!

The only other railway memory of that period was hearing the daily goods train through Fittleworth on its way to and from Midhurst whilst in the playground at school; most likely hauled by an E4 or C2X or perhaps a Q locomotive.

The local haulage contractor had a trio of elderly coaches for schools services and private hire, and these would be used for the occasional school outing. There was a pair of Commer Avengers and a Bedford OB. We had one of the Commers one day on a trip to Bognor Regis, and it really struggled on Bury Hill!

My mother's sister and husband had moved to Kent and we spent many summer holidays with them. At the beginning, it was back to the buses, journeying to Brighton and then taking the South Coast Express to Dover, which was quite a long trip as we always travelled on a Saturday when the roads were very congested, even then. This was a joint service operated by Southdown, East Kent and Royal Blue. I became very interested in the East Kent fleet, which at that time was quite varied and in a rich deep red and cream livery. The local service where we stayed was operated by rebuilt Dennis Lancets. The service, route 78, was infrequent and took us into Deal. In South Street, there was a small bus station where all buses had to reverse in, an inspector being provided to help with the movements. The town services operated from the middle of the road in South Street. A trip from Deal to Dover upstairs, front seat of course(!), could be quite exciting if the driver pulled out all the stops, as they seemed to mostly on the downhill so as to get a good run at the next uphill. The views out over the English Channel from the top deck were fantastic. Dover had a large bus garage, which was always well worth a visit, with vehicles quite different from those back home.

AEC Regent V's at East Kent bus station, Deal 30/8/1968

By 1965, I had started at the grammar school in Horsham, which entailed transport by bus and train each way. During the next six years, the local bus services became thinner on the ground and were converted to one-man operations. The fast train services were now in the hands of Kent coast stock (4CEP), but the stopping services were still in the hands of pre-war stock. On starting school in the September of 1965, the Horsham to Guildford line had recently closed but the Horsham to Brighton line still had a year to go, being operated by DEMUs and class 33 locomotives. Horsham station was still lit by gas lights at that time, and while waiting for the train home in the late afternoon there was generally a Three Bridges-bound train of loaded ballast hoppers from Meldon Quarry which passed through behind a class 70 'Hornby' electric locomotive. The science block at school was placed so that the windows overlooked the playing fields, and beyond them was Horsham goods yard, which was still relatively busy at this time so that I could look over and study the class 08 diesel shunter running up and down the yard. The first couple of years, there always seemed to be several former steam engine tenders for sludge transport, or maybe for use by Chipmans in their weed-killer trains, evident in the yard. The 08 also ran the thrice-weekly pick-up freight to Pulborough and Petworth, but that finished in the spring of 1966, these sightings fuelling my interest in railways.

London Transport ran some bus services from Horsham and, accompanied by a friend, I found that it was possible to purchase a so-called 'green rover ticket' which entitled us to travel on all London Transport country services. The ticket was issued from the conductor's machine and was about a yard long! We used it for a whole day and managed to reach Windsor in a rather roundabout way, seeing many places not seen before and sampling various types of vehicles.

In 1965, our local scout group summer camp was in Jersey. We travelled on the boat train from Waterloo, which at that time was still steam hauled to Weymouth. The ferries were run by British Rail and, being summer, they were packed with holidaymakers. We could see that the staff in the cafeteria were run off their feet, and being the good boy scouts that we were (!), we offered to help in clearing the tables. It turned out to be quite profitable as we could keep all the tips and got a lot to eat from the galley! We returned on the same ferry the following week, and the staff asked if we would do the honours again! Transport on the island was a bit of a museum piece, with quite a lot of elderly vehicles. I managed to get in a visit to the depot of Jersey Motor Transport and was shown around by the Traffic Manager. The JMT buses were in a livery very similar to that of Southdown; a bit like home from home.

Two years later, the summer camp was in Guernsey, this time with the boat trains being diesel-hauled as steam had just been phased out. Transport on the island was a bit like Jersey, with a mix of ancient and modern. The buses at that time were very much used, as in Jersey two years previously, and worked on the system of pay as you enter on the way into town, as St Peter Port was shown on the destination screen, and pay as you leave on the way out!

After leaving the scouts, I joined the combined cadet force at school, mainly to be able to get off classes now and again! It gave a good insight into the workings of the army, which confirmed my belief that to pursue a military career was not for me. In my time there, we were away on three summer camps, 1968–70. The first was in Suffolk, travelling from Liverpool Street to Ely behind a class 37 diesel and then on to Brandon in a DMU. This amused me as the guard came through checking tickets and was equipped with a 'Setright' ticket machine, just like the bus conductors back home. The next year took us to Okehampton to where we were transported by special train from Paddington. I remember that for our return journey we arrived in good time and sat on the platform to wait. The train duly arrived behind a 'Warship' class diesel-hydraulic, and the locomotive proceeded to run round the stock prior to shunting over to our platform. When the locomotive backed down onto the train, it made quite violent contact with the first carriage; so much so that the crew got down to inspect any eventual damage.All seemed to be well as we departed on time. For the third summer, we went to the Lüneburger Heide in Germany. We took the boat train from Liverpool Street to Harwich Town and sailed with Prinz Ferries to Bremerhaven. Even though it was summer, it was quite a rough crossing. The first sightings of DB trains around Bremen and Hannover awoke an interest in German railways that has remained with me to this day.

In 1970, I joined the Bluebell Railway station staff at Sheffield Park, moving to the locomotive department the following year, where I remained until 1977. At that time, there were not so many locomotives available for traffic; two SE & CR class P, the LB & SCR E4 and the GWR 'Dukedog'. Later, I also worked on the USA tank, Adams 'radial' tank, SE & CR class C and the standard class 4 locomotives. As a passed cleaner, one could get a firing turn nearly every Saturday and also quite often on Sundays as there were certain members of the department whom one could rely on not to turn up! Not having my own transport, it was getting increasingly difficult to get to and from Sheffield Park, so I made the decision to stop.

During the same period, I also got a bit involved in road transport preservation. I had a short acquaintance with the owner of a steam roller, during which I attended a couple of steam rallies and acted as steerer. There were also a couple of friends at Sheffield Park who had bought buses for preservation, one from Southampton and the other from Thames Valley. The Southampton bus was a Guy Arab III, on which some of us travelled to London to help the owner move from his London flat to one of the railway cottages at Sheffield Park; it was an unusual experience, using a double-decker bus on a removal job. The latter bus, owned by Stan, was a Bristol with a crash gearbox, and when we took it to a garage in Burgess Hill for an MOT test, the 'crashing' of gears had to be heard to be believed! Stan's arm was aching quite a lot when the day was over. The bus was used a few times to transport members of the locomotive department to local pubs on Saturday evenings, which caused a bit of a stir amongst the locals! He found a barn in Lewes where it could stand under cover and where we could begin to work on it, doing some preventive rust removal and painting. Sometimes, however, the call from Harvey's brewery was greater than that from the paintbrush! All this petered out when I left the Bluebell Railway.

Even though I had a great interest in road transport, and still have to a certain extent for anything built before 1970, the calling of the rails was the loudest.

218 290-3 Hof Hbf 31/10/1973

001 173-4 Bahnbetriebswerk Hof 31/10/1973

LSWR 488, Sheffield Park, summer 1974

Essex House

My time at school drew to an end in 1971. After a meeting with the careers master, an interview was arranged at Essex House, Croydon, with a successful outcome and a starting date of 23rd August.

Now came the day when I would begin my career as a professional railwayman. I started as a clerical officer of the lowest rank in the Rules Section on the 10th (top) floor. Soon after starting, I was sent to the Divisional Area Manager's Office at Beckenham to attend an introduction course comprising general information about British Rail's organisation with information concerning terms of employment and possibilities for educational courses and promotion.

The Rules Section dealt with a variety of subjects such as production of weekly engineering notices, amendments to rules/regulations, abolishment of signalboxes/amendments to signalbox workings, investigation of accidents/derailments, etc., and supply of stores for Area Signalling Inspectors/Station and Area Managers. All Signalling Inspectors were attached to the section where the Chief Inspector had his office, which was situated on the same floor.

My duties were, of course, of a menial nature but gave a good (or bad?) insight into the administrative workings of the railway. Most of my co-workers in the section were my senior by quite a number of years but seemed to accept a long-haired teenager in their midst! Some were career office staff, not practical railwaymen, and others were either redundant staff or there for health reasons. One, Arthur, who had been a guard for many years, took me under his wing. He was there because ill health had decreed a change of job. He was in charge of the stores, which were situated on the ground floor, and I was able to skive off now and again if he needed 'help'! We used to sit down there, where he related a lot of stories about his time out and about on the Central Division as both a goods and passenger guard! One day, he brought to my notice the fact that a Station Master's chair was offered for sale and did I want to make a bid? My finances were not that good as the job was rather poorly paid, but I put in a bid of one pound! After a couple of weeks, I received a telephone call from Stewarts Lane carriage and wagon department. I was told that my bid had been accepted and that the chair had been fully restored, and where should they send it to? It was put on a train to Pulborough for me to collect. It transpired that the chair had been found in the Yardmaster's office at Battersea Yard and that the initials LB & SC were carved in the back. I still have it to this day and value it most highly.

It did not take very long before I came into conflict with the section leader because of my appearance. He was a bit 'old school' and could not accept my style of clothing! It was too colourful and I should be more soberly dressed, so I went to my union, TSSA, who intervened on my behalf, and I won the day as the rule book stated only that one should be clean and presentable. After that, the atmosphere became a little cooler! Us juniors got quite a bit of overtime in as a new rule book was to be introduced. This was in loose-leaf form, and they all had to be put together before distribution. That did not go down too well, either, as the smell of our evening meals, fish and chips, etc., pervaded the whole office during that period, provoking some negative comments each morning as there had not been any airing of the rooms during the night.

Sometimes, I was put in to help in that part of the section which produced the weekly engineering notices, and there I came into contact with the Area Signalling Inspectors. As I had also begun evening classes for rules and regulations, they helped me a great deal with some of the intricacies of the rule book. Often on Fridays, they would take me with them for a pub lunch, not exactly following the rule book, but nobody seemed to take much notice!

During my time in the section there had been several derailments in the division, and each time, everybody was galvanised into action. There would be much studying of the rule book, with the intention of placing guilt. To me, it seemed rather unsavoury as it was very easy to sit in an office and read the rules, whereas out on the real railway split-second decisions had to be made. That is when I began to regret having started in administration as, in my opinion, everybody employed within British Rail had a role to play and should be regarded as equals, but that was not the case, there being an air of superiority amongst many of the office staff, who regarded practical railwaymen as of a much lower class.

I did have a chance to sit in on a Ministry of Transport inquiry into a collision at Horsham of a ballast train running into the rear of a passenger train, which was presided over by Major Olver. This was conducted at a very fair level, with all witnesses being questioned and heard by the inquiring officer without any direct accusations. Blame had, of course, to be found but also the reasons leading up to the event, such as perhaps the need for brush-up courses for staff or maybe an amendment to the rule book, any recommendations being published in the final report.

I was getting rather dissatisfied with my position and decided that now I wanted to be a real railwayman and therefore applied for the post of secondman at Redhill Motive Power Depot. I attended an interview at Redhill and after a medical was duly accepted. My seniority date would be 30th October 1972, and so the next ten years would involve getting out and about on the track.

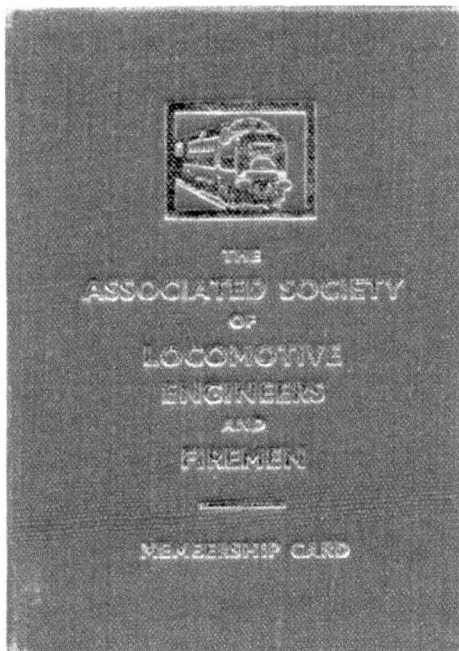

Redhill Mixed Traction Depot

30 October 1972. That date is most important as it was the seniority date for my entering the motive power department and used in connection with promotion and transfer between depots. After a short interview with the Area Depot Manager, I was accosted by the union representative and duly joined ASLEF, a move that I have never regretted as solidarity within the workforce is essential to be able to stand up for both pay and working conditions, and having a union alone for footplate staff means that we fought for our rights without drowning in the midst of a large general railway union.

Redhill depot at that time was still situated in what remained of the former steam shed, but early in 1973 we moved to a row of wooden huts situated nearer the station, which resulted in the saving of a few minutes' walking time on most duties. The depot was run by an area depot manager and an office staff of three, who were supported by three motive power supervisors and five shedmen. There was a complement of fifty drivers in two links of twenty-four and twenty-six, plus a shunting link of three, normally occupied by medically restricted men and a link of twenty-four secondmen. Traction was 'standard' southern region DEMUs, 08/09, 33 and 73, later also 47 and DMMUs. Booked workings took us regularly to Tonbridge, Woking, Reading, Didcot, Greenford, Willesden, Ardingly, Brighton and New Cross Gate, and special workings took us all over the division as there was a permanent way assembly depot at Three Bridges with which we were closely associated.

So now began a career that I thought would last until retirement, which later proved right but with modifications on the way. Traction training school at Waterloo South Sidings – what a dump! Rather run-down wooden buildings beside the approaches to Waterloo station, but the course included two practical weeks at our home depots and some days out, which helped. We had two instructors, Inspector Ted Lench from Salisbury and Inspector White from Eastleigh, who did their best to make the course interesting and to keep a group of twelve young men under control. We visited Hither Green depot to practice coupling locomotives in multiple, Stewarts Lane for fire practice and Elmers End to visit a signalbox. Otherwise, the course comprised lectures on rules and regulations, safety at work and a general background on the workings of the railway, finishing up with two days of exams. There followed an interview with the depot manager and I was now titled passed traction trainee as of 08/01/73 and then appointed secondman on 12/02/73, taking my place on the roster from that day. Before being placed on the roster, one was at the whim of the list clerk, which resulted in several days on loan to Norwood and various special freight turns. A lot of Norwood's work was classed as 'round the houses', but I did get a couple of good days out, one being a passenger turn from London Bridge to Uckfield and ECS to East Grinstead and another which involved both a passenger train to East Grinstead and a van train from Bricklayer's Arms Freight Depot to Guildford via Epsom and Effingham Junction.

There were seven weeks spare or ballast cover in the roster, but at that time we were never spare as there was a lot of trackwork going on, plus there was a multitude of aggregate trains run in connection with the building of the M23 and M25 motorways with terminals at Gatwick Airport and Merstham. Our booked workings were a mixture of passenger, parcels and aggregates, and there was a lot of night work, seven out of twenty-four weeks, and if one was not booked out Saturday night then it was easy to get an extra Sunday duty squeezed in to boost earnings, booked Sunday workings being few for secondmen. Rest day working at that time was also prevalent as there always seemed to be a short-age of staff; a result of too-drastic cutbacks maybe? One big problem I had was that living away from the depot, it was difficult getting in for early shifts and getting home off late evening shifts, so a great deal of swapping shifts took place. Luckily, shifts middle morning and, of course, nights were not always that popular, so it was often easy to get a changeover.

The drivers were a mixed bunch, varying in age from mid-thirties to late fifties, on the whole good to work with but as with all workplaces some odd exceptions who were not so easy to get on with. Several were original Redhill drivers, but there was also a large group who had come from Three Bridges when the mixed traction depot there closed in 1969, plus several transferred in from other regions to get promotion, so one also had to get used to various accents, although not nearly as bad as going on loan to Norwood Junction depot where there was a large contingent from Scotland, which could test one somewhat. Sometimes on arriving at the depot, it sounded as though one had come to Glasgow instead of south London!

To describe our duties in detail is difficult as the contents were constantly being altered, sometimes for no apparent reason, but we did have some that remained fairly constant in the time that I was at the depot. We had two night turns to Didcot, one of which we booked on at 20.38 taking over a class 73 electro-diesel that had come from Maidstone. The load was always just three to four vans, which was just as well having to run on diesel most of the way with just electric power from Redhill to Reigate, Shalford Junction through Guildford to Ash and again from Wokingham to Reading Spur Junction. We put off one van at Guildford and the rest at Reading in one of the west end bay platforms and then proceeded light engine to Didcot, originally working a van train to Basingstoke before heading for Didcot, but that was lost to the western region. Heads down for an hour and then we took over vans from South Wales for a 02.12 departure for Reading and home with a 04.56 arrival. Although the class 33 and 73 locomotives were fitted with aws, we only encountered it working when on other regions, the southern being somewhat behind in installation. Thus, one night, whilst with one of the older drivers, we were happily working towards Didcot light engine when we encountered a double yellow signal with associated warning horn. My driver started muttering whilst feverishly pressing the cancel button. All the while, I could hear the rear cab horn blasting away and as time ran out, the brakes went on and we stopped in a bit of a heap. Only then did my driver switch on the cab lights to find that it was the wrong button he had been pressing. He quickly and without a word reset the aws and we continued on our way, with me thinking that it would be prudent not to make any comment! This duty later became a class 33 job, with the locomotive doing a second trip to Didcot at 06.05. This day trip was only double-manned on Saturdays, giving a welcome journey there in daylight. Our other Didcot run was quite different as it was vans to Didcot then light to Reading to work the 06.47 passenger train to Redhill. Initially, we worked to Didcot via Guildford but then it was rerouted via East Croydon, Crystal Palace, Herne Hill, Clapham Jn (w) and then over the West London line to Old Oak Common and down the GW main line, which lasted for a year or two before being rerouted once again from Clapham Jn via Richmond and Ascot, so nothing was constant. On arrival back at Reading, we were coupled onto our train for pre-heating, where some of the drivers understood that it was assumed by the shunters that the secondman coupled on in return for free newspapers, but in my case they could assume again, which caused some initial discussion, ending with my driver doing the coupling! All stations back to Redhill after having been out all night could be a bit tedious, but some light relief could be had with some of the younger drivers, the job being in number two link. Around North Camp we would meet the first DEMU from Redhill, where we would duck down under the desk just to see our opposite number's reaction on seeing an apparently crewless locomotive, and on leaving Ash it would be full power to Wanborough so as to arrive with a couple of minutes in hand just to see the bowler hats running down the road!

My fortunes changed as regards travelling to and from work when I met Peter, a driver in the top link who took me under his wing, not only as regards learning the job but also inviting me to stay at his house in Redhill whenever I needed to and becoming a part of the family. We swapped turns whenever we could to be together, and I can honestly say that he taught me all I knew about rules and regulations, faults and failures and the actual driving of trains, where after a while we always shared the driving fifty-fifty, and it was because of him that I had no problem with passing my rules exam later on. The driving methods I learnt followed me to my second career, where I could pass them on to my trainees.

We had both an early and late turn on class 08 working trips between Redhill and Merstham and Holmethorpe sand siding. The sand siding was so steep that the load was restricted to about nine loaded hoppers, plus brake van, and on leaving the siding we engaged the series only switch so that we could keep a constant traction output without the locomotive trying to change to parallel working. The trips were classified as class 9 unfitted workings and were good training for brake control and for shunting. The late turn also involved shunting Redhill Goods, which was situated at Earlswood, and then working a heavy trip of mixed freight to Redhill Up Yard in preparation for the evening departure to Norwood Junction, which was always a full load for a class 33.

Ballast workings had nominal allotted times of 0400, 0900, 2100 and 2200, although the other spare turns would also be utilised if necessary. All spare turns could be moved up to two hours either side of the rostered time. We covered mostly the middle part of the central division as Brighton and Norwood covered respectively the coastal and London parts, so a lot of our work was centered on Tonbridge – Redhill – Guildford, Coulsdon North – Redhill –Three Bridges – Horsham – Arundel and Horsham – Dorking – Epsom and sometimes on the Oxted lines but of course could be utilised elsewhere on the division, a trip to Newhaven with a train of spent ballast often being integrated into a diagram.

The night turns would usually start with collecting our train at Three Bridges, sometimes New Cross Gate, and then working to the site with a return by taxi in the early hours, getting relief by an early turn arriving by taxi. That was not always as easy as it appeared on paper because some drivers liked to stretch the job out to make overtime and would try to arrange for the train to be as far away as possible from the booked relieving point, which would sometimes involve tramping across fields in all weathers and pitch dark! Other drivers would make just as much overtime by agreeing with the relieving driver a fictive time of relief! The 0900 ballast turn could be utilised for a multitude of tasks such as spent ballast to Newhaven, collecting long welded rail at Chichester, etc. The guards' route learning saloon was another such duty which could involve covering most of the southern half of the division. One night, as so often happened, we were to start with a class 73 light engine to Three Bridges to pick up our train. Whilst walking from the mess room to the loco sidings, the skies opened up and we were soaked through, so after starting the diesel engine we took off most of our clothing to drape it over the engine to try and dry it out. I have often wondered what the travelling public thought on seeing an apparently naked crew passing through!

We were at New Cross Gate one night to pick up a ballast train and were in the shunters' lobby awaiting the arrival of our guard, who eventually appeared in a rather irate state of mind and proceeded to ring control, demanding another brake van to the one he was allocated as there was excreta on the floor! The controller obviously asked him to repeat what he had said but still did not seem to understand the problem, to which the guard in exasperation said, 'Fxxxing shit to you,' before terminating the conversation. The head shunter quietly said that he could have just asked him instead of putting his blood pressure at risk and then requested us to do a simple shunt move to swap the brake van. The guard had now calmed down somewhat, and we could continue with the diagrammed duty.

Today, it seems incredible that in the early '70s we were still working freight trains with either unfitted or partially fitted brakes; something unheard of on the Continent. I have never understood the logic when one thinks about the vast amounts of capital invested in the railways after nationalisation and the powers at be just continuing with out-of-date methods.

Whilst many of the ballast jobs were very similar in content, there did crop up something a little different, like working a class 08 from Horsham to Dorking and returning with a couple of open wagons with granite chippings for filling up the lineside bins; it took all night – a long night! Then a Saturday afternoon doing two trips from Holmethorpe sand siding to Three Bridges with double-headed 08s.

More interesting were the excursion specials that turned up during the summer months. The Southern Region often utilised six-car 'Hastings' DEMUs of the 6B variant (buffet car) far and wide, being worked by central division crews throughout, as although Western Region drivers were trained on DEMUs, they would not take the six-car units for some vague reason, which of course was good for us.

One Saturday, Peter and I were booked to travel as passenger on the 09.34 to Reading and then on to Cheltenham to work a return excursion. The outward journey left Redhill about 08.55 and we suggested to the other crew that we could work it both ways and they could take an unofficial day off, to which they readily agreed, keeping well out of the way of the foreman! It was a most interesting day out with a Gloucester pilot driver from Reading and returning with several hours in Cheltenham to look around the town and getting paid for it. Peter had been one of a small group of drivers to be trained on DMMUs for working the ultra-sonic test train, which resulted in a trip from Kensington Olympia to Hastings with a ten-car set and another day two trips to Reading and return because of a shortage of our own units. I was also initiated in driving these units, which was something completely new, with vacuum brakes and gear changing! The six-car DEMUs would also put in an appearance whenever it was Farnborough Air Show to increase capacity, the diagrams having to be carved up once again to mitigate the problem of Western drivers refusing to work them, necessitating the provision of a secondman – an example duty being two trips to Reading and one to Tonbridge.

Inter-regional workings could also show up a complete lack of logical planning as one Saturday afternoon showed. We were booked to pick up a class 33 at Three Bridges and run light to Horsham, where we collected a Chipman weed killer train destined for Stratford. We were routed via Dorking to Kensington Olympia, where on arrival we waited for a pilot driver and guard who duly arrived with a light class 25 which they parked in one of the bay platforms. We then proceeded via Willesden HL, Gospel Oak, Canonbury and Victoria Park, leaving the train in Stratford Old Yard and returning light engine via Temple Mills, South Tottenham to Gospel Oak and then Kensington, where we could drop off the Willesden men so that they could return home with their loco and we could continue to Selhurst depot for fuel. It was an interesting day out for us but a complete waste of resources as we could have come off our train at Kensington for the Willesden crew to continue to Stratford.

Another expensive working was one we had during the summer of 1975 on Saturdays, when we were booked to take a class 33 from Redhill loco sidings to Eastbourne. On arrival, we waited for an incoming SAGA holiday excursion to place our loco on the rear and then changeover with the one that had arrived and work back light to Redhill! Nice run out but what did it cost? We had a regular job with a sand train to Greenford which had a very social booking on time of 08.15, which gave a daylight run over the West London Line and then out via Acton and Ealing Broadway before turning onto the Greenford loop. After depositing the train, some drivers preferred to get away with the empties as quickly as possible, whereas others would go to the staff canteen at the glass works where one could get a good hot dinner for a very reasonable price. On leaving Greenford, we continued past Park Royal and then again Old Oak Common and West London. We were then booked via Crystal Palace and after picking up more empties at Norwood Junction proceeded to Merstham yard, where all the wagons would be shunted in. On one occasion on arrival at Merstham, there came no signal from the guard's brake van, so the driver sent me back to find that there was no guard! We shunted in, and on arrival back at the depot, the foreman informed us that the guard had dropped off to make some tea after giving us the new loadings. There was, of course, a question of exchanging hand signals on departure from Norwood, or lack of them, but the driver had to explain that. There were several destinations for the fine sand from Holmethorpe, being Queenborough, Harlow Mill, St Helens and Pontypool, as well as Greenford.

In the autumn of 1973, Peter and I took a trip to West Germany via the Harwich to Hook of Holland ferry. Our destination was Hof and Marktredwitz to see the last rites of steam working. The regular class 001 pacific workings had finished earlier in the year but were still on standby, plus a handful of 086 tank locos and, of course, the ubiquitous class 050. Trains from the DDR would come over the border with Deutsche Reichsbahn locomotives, which would return very quickly to the east. We had acquired shed passes, which gave us a free hand to wander around, and at Marktredwitz, which was a small sub-shed of Hof, we were invited onto the footplate of their 01 stand-by locomotive, where the crew proceeded to show off by thrashing up and down the shed yard. We also visited the shed at Schwandorf but as we had no permit were abruptly ejected but managed to get round to see the locos anyway! My interest in German railways was really established here.

It was about this time that link number one was trained on the class 47, the main reason being that instead of a class 52 being changed over for a 33 at Redhill, the 47 would work throughout to Ardingly. To give the drivers more experience with them, the depot was also allocated an aggregate train to Gatwick Airport, returning the empties to Woking. This did not go down too well with Basingstoke depot as until then they had a monopoly of these workings. At this time the four-digit headcodes were still used, and with several run-rounds, a lot of time was spent winding the blinds. We also began to get some excursion traffic with class 47. The aggregate workings for the motorway construction were beginning to be run down now, and coupled with the loss of our sand train working to Greenford after the closure of the glass works we began to have more days sitting spare at the depot. Generally speaking, a day spare could be quite entertaining. One day, a certain driver asked where he could get a load of shit for his garden! There was no end to the suggestions. The same driver also complained one day that he had no onion to go with his sandwiches. The next morning, he was presented with an onion about the size of a cricket ball. Upon asking where it came from, he got the reply – the signalman's allotment behind Longhedge Jn signalbox and that as it was dark at the time, one could not see how big they were! The depot mess room was shared by both the mixed traction and the EMU depots. One of the EMU drivers, Frank Hall, came in one day and proclaimed that a vacancy had occurred. On perusing the roster, the 'H' was missing from Frank's name, so it showed F All! He used to cycle to work and if it was raining he had a newspaper stuffed inside his jacket, and when he made the tea it was what was called a 'Bricklayer's Arms twist': tea, sugar and condensed milk wrapped in greaseproof paper, which was plopped into boiling water. During this period, there were still many that liked a pint of beer if the opportunity arose. One day, waiting to travel home as passenger from Guildford, my driver and I decided to have a quick one. We had just got our drinks when a fight broke out and we ducked down behind the juke box whilst chairs flew around the bar, until the police arrived and we could creep out and get off home. There was also a late turn, which was two return trips to Reading, the first with a DEMU and the second with a class 33, where we berthed the stock at Reading and returned light engine, although previously I believe the loco had been utilised for working empty oil tanks from North Camp to Redhill and thence to the Isle of Grain refinery.

With certain drivers, the idea was to make a quick run as far as Chilworth so that there was time for a pint before the section cleared, the signalman often giving us the tip when it was time to go! One of the shedmen had a bit of a drink problem and would often go over to the pub just outside the depot for a pint, which could amount to several during the course ofan evening. He had a drinker's red face and as he returned one night, the foreman looked out of the window and commented that he had the red shades up, comparing his face to the tail lights on the multiple unit stock! Gladly, it became more and more unacceptable to drink whilst on duty. Another shedman had a false leg and could always be heard approaching, as it squeaked a lot, and one day he sank to the ground outside the foreman's office with metal fatigue! When there were periods with several spare men on duty together, there would be darts matches or a card school. I managed to stop one game of cards by discreetly setting fire to an oily wiper in a metal waste bin and sliding it in under the table, thereby smoking the players out! Some of the drivers could be rather uncouth. One especially would often let off wind, leaving no alternative than to open the cab windows, whatever the weather might be. He did this quite noisily one day in the messroom whilst a Littlehampton driver was on his break. He reacted, quite understandably, by saying in a rather indignant voice, 'Do you mind! I'm having my grub,' but he got no response.

In the autumn of 1974, Peter and I took another trip to Germany, this time to Rheine and Emden in the north. Again, we had shed passes which we used to the full. There were not many steam-hauled passenger services left, but an endless stream of freight trains, mainly coal and iron ore, many of which were double-headed, operated between the two stations, taking over from electric power at Rheine. The locomotives were mainly oil-fired classes 042, 043 and 011, plus some 050 and at Emden a few 094 heavy shunters.

Back home, we returned to the daily routines. We had a late-turn passenger job booking on at 17.38 to prepare a class 33 and work 18.41 to Tonbridge and then 19.45 through to Reading, returning with 23.25 to Guildford. The make-up of the train then became interesting as the Guildford pilot added some parcel vans onto the rear plus a goods brake van as our loco-hauled sets (TSO/BSK/TSO/GUV) were air-braked and the vans were vacuum braked, so now it was ECS + vans to Redhill at 45mph. At one point, we were in dispute with management, which happened from time to time(!), and one night on arrival at Guildford we received not only the parcels vans but also two DEMU sets that had been taken out of service earlier and had to be returned to Redhill for further movement to St Leonards depot. We were booked relief on arrival at Redhill, so it was not us that had to sort that lot out. The duty was a good one for trying a bit of cooking as we had an hour at Reading before departure. On the class 33 there was a small cooker in the engine room, so jacket potatoes put in at Redhill and a pie at Guildford were just the ticket. We also used it whilst out on ballast jobs, when there were often long periods of inactivity. Some of these duties could be quite boring if you were with the 'wrong' driver who wasn't particularly talkative, so a book was always in my bag.

At this time, my enthusiasm for the job was such that I had a couple of trips with Peter on my day off (!) whilst he was on a duty to St Leonards (West Marina) diesel depot. The first was on the night turn which ran to exchange the DEMU sets used on the Tonbridge to Reading service, the so-called 'tadpole' units, which were made up of two 'Hastings gauge' vehicles coupled with an ex-EMU driving trailer built to normal loading gauge. The service ran as a mail train from Redhill to Hastings, returning thus to the depot via the carriage washer and fuel point. The return ran as ECS to Eastbourne and then as a staff train to Redhill. The trains usually comprised two units but often conveyed extras as required.

The second occasion was on the day turn, which was normally covered by the second link which started by travelling passenger to Purley to relieve a Tunbridge Wells West driver and running as ECS all the way to St Leonards, although at the height of the summer season it ran as an extra passenger service to Eastbourne. The return was also ECS except Eastbourne to Haywards Heath, which ran as a school train. These services comprised three Oxted/Hampshire sets. St Leonards depot was primarily for the maintenance of DEMU sets, although I think that the twelve Hastings line 'Cromptons', later class 33/2, were initially allocated there, plus a couple of Drewry class 04 diesel shunters that had taken over the freight working to Tenterden Town at the end of the 1950s. The depot was used period-ically for classified maintenance of class 33 as I witnessed on the day turn, when there was ample time to look around and there happened to be a 'Crompton' in the lifting shed.

The cabs of our locomotives, except for class 47, were not particu-larly comfortable if one was sitting about for any length of time as not being able to adjust the seats backwards, one could only stretch out over the control desk, resulting in 'dead' legs after a short while. If there was no prospect of having to move for some time then we locked the doors and stretched out on the floor. Heating was okay, but I did experience one night after the Christmas shutdown when we were booked light engine to Reading to fetch the 06.47 passenger train. We started the engine about one and a half hours before depar-ture as there was ice on the inside of the windows but still had to keep our overcoats on most of the night as it never really warmed up properly. Class 33 failures were few and far between, but one after-noon on the 16.40 passenger from Redhill when getting the 'right away' from Wanborough, nothing happened. Upon opening the controller everything appeared to be fine, with all fuses and circuit breakers intact, engine running and plenty of air, but it just would not take power. We telephoned the signalman to declare us a failure, who informed us that the next train behind us was an EMU that could propel us to Ash, where it could run round us to continue to Aldershot and then the following DEMU could push us to North Camp and into the up siding there. This is what happened, whereupon we shut the engine down and returned home on the cushions. That was the only time that I experienced a failed train as a secondman but was out several times with a loco to rescue others.

I have recorded about twenty different drivers who would let me have a drive, some sharing fifty-fifty and some letting me do it all. If on shunting duty, especially the pilot at Three Bridges, then the driver would remain in the lobby and let you get on with it. I have also experienced waiting at Redhill home signal and the driver announcing that he wanted to get a particular train home and then disappear, leaving me to take the locomotive onto the loco sidings, which involved running into the station and then via Earlswood. I had by this time unofficially obtained a master control key. One driver who would never hand over the controls on the main line would often let one shunt, for example, with parcel vans into the bay platform at Reading, as if it was some great honour.

During the time I was at Redhill there were several disputes with management but generally just odd days on strike. One day, together with my driver, I relieved a Norwood driver at Selhurst on a train of empty oil tanks for Willesden. Arriving at the locomotive, the driver to be relieved gave up the information regarding the train's weight, length, etc., but my driver did not reply. When we had settled in the cab, I asked him what had just gone on, whereupon he replied that that particular driver had worked in the 1955 strike(!) and he had refused to speak to him ever since. This was in 1974! Feelings always ran high with such conflicts, quite understandably, in my opinion. I experienced the same Norwood driver a couple of times when sent on loan there. He seemed to have a high opinion of himself and always had plenty to say and was known at the depot as 'Shovel Gob'. One early morning, my driver, Keith Fagan, and I arrived on the reception road at Norwood Up Yard and screwed the handbrake on as our time was up, having been out on a ballast working all night. The aforementioned driver was the relief foreman at Norwood that night and came rushing out to say that our train was in the way and that he had no one to move it and that we could not just leave it there, to which Keith said, 'Just watch us,' and we walked off towards the station with the foreman practically jumping up and down in a rage. Nicknames were common at that time, and there were several at Redhill, some examples being as follows – The Vicar, Mum, Speedy, Porky, Bootsie, Clinker, Slash, Wank, Randy Reg and The Colonel amongst others. Some were obvious, whereas others could be rather obscure.

One night, after leaving a class 33 in Redhill Up Yard, my hand slipped whilst climbing down and I caught my thumb in the door. I did not think much of it at the time, but when I came into the warm lobby from the frost degrees outside, it began to hurt quite a bit. The foreman that night was Cyril White and seeing that there was a blood blister under the nail, he applied pressure and dispersed it. Then it was off to the doctor, and I got it bound up with the promise that I would lose the nail. A sequel to this was that the next night on the same duty, Didcot vans, we pulled in on the down through line at Reading alongside another van train. I was driving so was next to the secondman on the class 50, who leant out to hear if I could help him roll a cigarette, lifting his arm at the same time to show that his thumb was bound up after he had caught it in a cab door the previous night. This caused much merriment to our respective drivers.

On the Didcot night jobs we used the mess rooms either at Didcot or Reading diesel depot, where we never felt that we were particularly welcome, the arrangement appearing to be one table for the local crews, one for other western region crews and a third for 'foreign' crews; something we were generally not used to on the southern, except at Victoria, where there was a distinct central and south eastern division. I always thought it rather strange as we all worked for the same company and did the same work, but I suppose that was just human nature. Another exception on the southern was Woking. We had for a period obtained a new night duty which involved booking on at 23.30 and then travel as passenger to Woking via Clapham Jn and Waterloo. We then had about an hour to wait for our train, and nobody seemed to want to have anything to do with us. It was a bit of an odd duty as we then relieved on a class 33 with a full load of aggregates from Westbury and worked it to Tonbridge West Yard, travelling as passenger back to Redhill. It was a heavy train and in the dip between Betchworth and Reigate, it was very difficult to avoid a snatch, whichever driving method was used. Apparently, we got the job because Tonbridge depot had tried to hold out to be trained on the class 47, but management insisted that it should remain class 33 hauled. The ultimate destination was Allington and the empties returned via London so once again a piece of bad diagramming as it could have been made an out-and-back job.

Promotion time was now approaching and on 30th January 1976, I was sent to Southern House at Croydon for a medical, which I duly passed. I then received a letter stating that I was required to attend a rules examination at Essex House on Saturday, 14th February at 09.30. This would be with Motive Power Inspector George Taylor and lasted six hours, minus an hour for lunch. It was a nearly 100% oral exam, the one exception being the thirteen instances of when one could pass a signal at danger, which one was allowed to write down. Having passed the exam, the next step was to find out if one should apply for a driver's vacancy straight away or remain at Redhill as a passed secondman.

Having plans to get married the following summer, I applied a bit reluctantly for a driver's vacancy at Dorking North (Central) depot for which I was successful, with a starting date of 5th April, so now there were not many days left on mixed traction duties. At that time, there would not be the possibility of a driving job at Redhill for the foreseeable future, so therefore my choice fell for the electrics. As it turned out, Redhill depot was expanded within the next few years, but by then I was established at Horsham with a house close to the depot. Looking at my notes, I can see that the last days at Redhill were the usual mixture of ballast duties and odd jobs. One was a return excursion coming from the West Country, which we relieved at Reading, working it to Eastbourne and ECS back as far as Redhill.

26

It was 33025 and ten coaches, and on arrival at Reading the tour leader came up to inform us that there had been no heating since Exeter! We assumed that the relieving driver at Exeter was not aware that when the master key was removed then the heating was also cut off and should be started again after inserting the new key, so we duly started the heating, receiving no further complaints!

On arrival at Redhill and running round, we were all set to go when a passenger came up who we knew to be a box boy at Gatwick Airport signalbox. He asked if we could stop at Three Bridges to drop him off, to which he received a rather sharp reply; we were only booked to stop at Haywards Heath, Lewes and all stations to Eastbourne. I then received notice to attend the driver training school at Waterloo South Sidings for electric multiple unit training. If I remember rightly, we were eight on the course and our instructor was acting Inspector Colin Marshall. The course was just three weeks to cover 1948, 1951, 1955 and 1963 stock, plus motor luggage vans, so it was relatively intense as none of us knew much about electric units. There was a mixture of classroom and practical days and we got about quite a bit as we had to find the different types of units, the first days out with the Westinghouse brake being a bit hairy. We also had a day at Stewarts Lane for training with the short circuiting bar and fire extinguishers. At the weekends I got in a Sunday shift, each time on ballast workings. The last two days of the course were examination days, one theory and one practical, two men at a time taking turns to answer the questions; if one failed to answer correctly, the question went over to the other victim. Our examining Inspector was George Bowman from Dover, who appeared to not suffer fools lightly. On the table in front of us was a driver's brake valve from a 4SUB unit which we had to use to show where the compressed air came from and went to, etc. The questions started off quite harmlessly, with general knowledge of the different types of stock, then graduating to braking systems. My opposite number faltered with one question which I then answered, but when he could not answer the next question, he was informed that he could not be used further that day and would have to come back another time! Shit, now I was on my own but managed to get through the rest of the day but realised that I would also be on my own for the practical exam the next day.

I was instructed to meet in the staff canteen at Victoria at 08.30 the next day, and after a coffee we went out to find some trains to work. The first was an 8SUB all stations to Coulsdon North, which went off quite well, with me managing to stop at the eight-car mark each time without too much trouble. Into the sidings at Coulsdon, where I was put through berthing and preparation procedures and also some fault finding and a practical demonstration of paddling up collector shoes and changing shoe fuses. We then walked to Coulsdon South and worked a 4VEP to Victoria, having lunch in the canteen there. After lunch, we walked to the carriage shed at Victoria (Eastern), where I had to show how to prepare a twelve-car rake of Kent Coast stock and then prepare an MLV, when I also had to demonstrate how I would work it with vacuum-fitted vans in tow. I thought we were now finished but, alas no; it was back to the station to work a 2EPB over the South London line to London Bridge, where on arrival Inspector Bowman shook my hand , wished me luck and handed over an EP-key proclaiming that I could now call myself a train driver. I was completely drained! I now had just one week left at Redhill, and that was a week of five nights on the Willesden vans and then I was finished with diesel locomotives, or so I thought.

My transfer day was 5th April, when I first had to report to Chief Motive Power Inspector George Holloway at Essex House and then Area Depot Manager Gordon Burrows at Redhill, who would still be my boss, also on transferring later to Horsham, so there was some continuity. I then travelled to Dorking to meet the leading driver at the depot and be allotted a locker, etc.

DEMU 1036,
Cheltenham, 3/8/74

47 151, 13/8/74 by
Three Bridges

47 151, Gatwick
M25 siding, 13/8/74

Redhill Loco Sidings, 25/8/74

33 038, Redhill Loco Sidings, 25/8/74

Driver's desk, 33 038, Redhill, 25/8/74

33 038, Redhill Loco, 25/8/74

47 096, 28/8/74, Kenneth Peter Oxlade, mentor and friend

*Another favourite driver, Roger
Pickthall, 33 059, 16.40 Redhill to Reading passenger train, 20/9/74*

Essex House
College Road
Croydon CR9 1NY
Tel 01-686 3422 Extn. 2972

D.C.R. MACKMURDIE

F. Paterson Divisional Manager Central Division

Driver A. Evans,
Redhill MT for Dorking (C).

y/r
o/r   SW 7 (MP)   31st March 1976

Dear Mr. Evans,

    You have qualified as capable of performing
the full duties of a driver Electric Multiple
Unit Traction, and I am pleased to inform you
that you have been certified as fit to be entrusted
with the responsibilities of that status.

    I feel you will appreciate the importance of
maintaining your knowledge and acting always in a
careful and conscientious manner in the performance
of your new duties.

    At this important stage of your career, I wish
you every good fortune for the future.

                          Yours sincerely,

                          J. GREENFIELD
                          MOTIVE POWER OFFICER

BR 14300/797

Promotion to driver letter 31/3/76

Dorking/Horsham Driver

Dorking North was a bit special as there were two drivers' depots, one for the central division, which had an establishment of ten, and one for the south west division, which had fourteen drivers but the guards covered both sides. We shared the same mess room, and the stock diagrams were spread over both divisions and comprised just 1948 (4SUB) units, so now there was ample chance to practise using the Westinghouse brake. The work was just suburban, with one job going south to Horsham, so both depots had common ground Horsham – Dorking – Epsom, from where we went our separate ways.

The next three months were mostly involved with route learning, so on 6th April I reported to Inspector Pratt at Victoria, who planned which routes to learn and in which order, leaving us alone to find out which trains to ride on, only insisting on fixed booking-on times. The first route was the direct line to Victoria via Sutton, Streatham Jn and Balham, followed by Sutton to Balham via West Croydon and Crystal Palace/via Selhurst. The depots at Selhurst and Streatham Hill were also included, Selhurst not being a special favourite of mine, having to take great care over conflicting movements and shunters who seemed to assume that the drivers could manage a lot of the movements without their help, so if one was uncertain then it was just a matter of waiting until a shunter eventually wandered down from their lobby. We reported once a week to Inspector Pratt to keep him up to date on our progress and to sign off routes as and when we were ready. After I had signed the first routes, which by then also included London Bridge 'rounders', both via Peckham Rye/Tulse Hill and via Forest Hill, then the Foremen at Selhurst, Victoria and London Bridge were aware of my presence, which often resulted in being taken off route learning to cover duties or parts of duties that were uncovered, therefore prolonging the training period. Inspector Pratt got a bit pissed off with that, but I eventually finished route learning on 9th July and could then take up my place on the roster. But first, summer holidays, which involved a trip to Denmark for my wedding, my future wife being Danish and wishing to be married in her home country.

As previously mentioned, we were ten drivers on the central division, with six diagrammed jobs and four weeks' spare/rest day relief. Problems with travel to and from work had cropped up again as we were living with my parents until we found a house in Horsham. But, my luck was in as one of the early turns had been altered to a 09.20 booking on time, which nobody else on my shift was interested in, particularly two of my colleagues who had window cleaning businesses on the side, so I was able to strike a deal which meant that if I took the 09.20 job for them then they would take the late turn, which finished after the last train to Horsham had departed, and that is what happened during all my time at Dorking.

The work was 90% 1948 stock work, with a single return working to Beckenham Jn with EPB stock on the late turn and a London Bridge 'rounder' on an early turn. We had a rather intensive duty on the late turn, which began by working to Victoria to attach and then to West Croydon via Crystal Palace, West Croydon to London Bridge via Forest Hill, and then a long 'rounder' via Forest Hill, Selhurst, Streatham Common, Tulse Hill and Peckham Rye. Arriving at London Bridge, a well-earned break and then a short 'rounder', also with 8SUB via Peckham Rye, Tulse Hill, Crystal Palace and Forest Hill, followed by a 4SUB to Horsham via Peckham Rye, Tulse Hill, Sutton and Dorking. The best for me was that on arrival at Horsham we were to travel back to Dorking as passenger, so I saved quite a bit of time each day. So much for later demands for being more efficient; we were already there in the 1970s! Otherwise, the work was a bit tedious, and according to my notes there were only two days with something out of the ordinary. One was a Sunday where I was booked passenger to Victoria to conduct south east division trains to and from Beckenham Junction as they were diverted via the central because of engineering work. These were main line stock, as was the second instance when, spare on a Saturday, I was called to travel to Horsham and conduct a Brighton driver to Victoria via Dorking and Sutton, who had been put on the job at the last moment. One incident which comes to mind was while working a Victoria to Beckenham Junction service with EPB stock; on leaving Streatham Hill tunnel, I saw a cricket bat placed longitudinal on top of one rail and was unable to stop in time. It worked like a ramp luckily splitting under the train's weight, but it gave quite a jolt.

People dumping rubbish over the fence onto the railway was quite a problem in the London area, although it was not unknown in country areas either. Throwing bicycles or other metal objects onto the conductor rail seemed to be a perverse form of humour at times. It now came to my notice that Colin Marshall, my instructor at the driving school, had been permanently appointed and thus his position at Horsham was vacant. I put in an application for the job and received notification that I was to transfer to Horsham depot as of 8th February 1977. So now it was a visit to Inspector Pratt again for a route-learning plan. This time, main lines to Littlehampton, Bognor Regis and Portsmouth Harbour, plus the branch to Three Bridges and Purley to Brighton via both Redhill and the Quarry Line and then from Brighton to Littlehampton. That took a month without interruptions, and then on signing all routes, the Inspector told me to disappear for a week and then take up my duties on 27th March, so a nice little bonus holiday.

The work at Horsham was a mixture of main line and suburban, with a fair amount of stock being stabled overnight, usually around seventeen four-coach units. The carriage sidings were spread around the station area, generally with a walking allowance of five minutes, but those furthest away were the 'branch sidings', which were situated alongside the line towards Three Bridges and had an allowance of twenty-five minutes. The 'malthouse siding' was south of the station and was also used as a headshunt from the down sidings. The train crew room was situated on the down platform in the former refreshment room and was shared with the guards. There were thirty-four drivers at that time, the majority being original Horsham steam men and the average seniority date being therefore quite high as we were only three that had been taken on since 1963. The depot was under the administration of the Area Depot Manager at Redhill, but the daily working came under the Motive Power Foreman at Brighton, whom we contacted by telephone when booking on for a spare turn. On the early turn, we had a 'cover' turn at 04.00 to cut-in heaters on some of the stock and then act as standby for anyone ringing in sick or sleeping over. This was later moved back to 03.15 so that we could cut-in all units. If everybody booked on to time and nothing was heard from Brighton, then one went home about 09.00! Several of the older fraternity were not too keen on the 'cover' job as it was a bit too early, so there were ample chances for swapping duties, for although it was very early, it was like being part-time employed. We took it upon ourselves to prepare all the outgoing trains and bring several of them into the platforms so that our colleagues could relax with a coffee before departure, this being done in co-operation with the signalman and station shunter.

So now I settled into the daily routines with the advantage of also having main line work. We worked alternate early and late duties, and therefore the depot was divided into two shifts of seventeen drivers. On our shift it was rare that the 'cover' man had to go out because of someone not turning up. If one lived close by, as I did, then there would be heavy banging on the front door to wake one up to avoid a trip to London! This happened a couple of times for me as we had no telephone installed for the first years of living there. There was a station supervisor on early and late shifts who was also a form of contact between us and the Brighton Foreman and Control. One of them was of a rather nervous disposition and at times of stress would get in quite a panic. He was once seen heading in a great rush for the toilets and calling out that he did not think he was going to make it, which was a rather pathetic sight but caused some merriment in the crew room! Another of the supervisors would always be on the look-out if there was a spare crew to get them something to do, and if there was some extra stock in the sidings, then look out, because he would soon have arranged for it to be removed! He came into the mess room one afternoon to ask who the pxxxk was that had knocked off the car park barrier the previous night. It was one of our colleagues who had forgotten his parking card and had tried to drive out immediately behind another colleague, but the barrier came down more quickly than he expected, with the result lying on the tarmac! This particular Inspector lived behind the 'malthouse siding' and announced one morning that he had received a load of turkey shit for his garden, but he had not needed to tell us because everyone who had been in the vicinity could smell it. The rest of the platform staff were a mixed bunch and one morning, whilst booking on, I enquired as to who was on the platform that morning, to which I got the reply, 'Old Scratch-arse.' It was an older railman who apparently had a bit of a problem; I had seen him several times standing in the shadows where in silhouette his trouser legs could be seen working up and down as he scratched away. It was very easy to acquire a nickname.

The incoming stock would be berthed in the same sidings everyday as shown on our diagrams so that all morning departures would also be in the same positions. There would occasionally be a shortage of units if there had been some incident the previous evening, which would result in gross overloading on some rush-hour trains, as if they were not already overloaded with a normal formation. When working 4SUB units, there was no form of communication between driver and guard, and therefore the 'right away' was given by a green flag or handlamp, which of course necessitated sticking one's head out of the window to see the guard, with the result that if one was a unit short then one stopped at the four-car mark, thus getting a lot of comments from the passengers who had been waiting further along the platform, but then one could decide to stop at the eight-car mark at some of the stations so that the guard got his share of the flak!

The driving cabs of the SUB-stock were not exactly the height of comfort, but for me the use of the Westinghouse brake always gave some interest to the job as with eight cars and platforms of just eight-car length then accuracy was the order of the day and could sometimes be a bit of a challenge, coupled with the desire to achieve as smooth a stop as possible. One became quite an expert after a while and could run hard into the platform with the desired result. I do not think that they would be passed as fit for service in these modern times, with no speedometers, oil-lit taillamps, barely lit stencil headcodes, where you either stood on one of the buffers or opened the offside front window to change them, practically no illumination in the brake gauges and line voltage in the cab! When berthing said units then one would listen for the compressor to stop before pulling the knife switch out, thus averting arcing! We sometimes made an agreement with the guard that we would not wait for running customers in the morning rush hour because then they would make sure to be on time the rest of the week. Outside the rush hour, one would usually wait unless already behind time.

For every timetable change there would be alterations to our diagrams, sometimes for the better and other times not so. On starting at Horsham, we had one duty which gave a mileage bonus, which later increased to three duties on weekdays plus a couple at weekends, which resulted in some colleagues speculating on when they would have their holidays so as not to lose the bonus to a spare man. These 'mileage' jobs kept one busy but the time passed quickly, and I quote two examples here: an early turn starting Horsham –London Bridge –Brighton, then Brighton –Portsmouth –Barnham –Bognor – Barnham –Littlehampton –Horsham and then on the late shift: Horsham – Portsmouth –Victoria via Horsham followed by Victoria–Horsham –Littlehampton –Horsham. This late turn was a bit hard, having to pass the depot for a second time, but one could always dash in to get a coffee before continuing southwards. We had several turns in the evenings and especially at the weekends, which involved two return trips to Victoria with a break at Horsham; living so close to the depot, I could eat at home.

Working at an EMUT depot was not as eventful as at an MT depot as most of the work was predictable, with the exception of a spare day or disruption caused by an operating incident or track engineering work, this latter especially at weekends. Breakdowns with electric stock were also few and far between, and during the six and a half years that I was driving I was involved in only three failures; funnily enough, two of them occurring within three months of each other in 1977.

The first was with the 12.35 empty stock working from New Cross Gate down sidings to Horsham, a booked weekday working which ran via West Croydon, Sutton and Dorking. On this day, 11th August, I prepared the train, which comprised4CIG 7435 and 4BIG 7032 and departed on time, but on coming out onto the down slow line and starting on the incline towards Brockley there was a distinct lack of power and we came to an involuntary standstill at Brockley platform. After notifying the signalman, I tried changing the power jumpers between the two sets, but it made no difference. The rear unit was apparently dead, so I declared the train a failure and awaited instructions. The signalman informed me that the yard shunter would be sent from New Cross Gate, so I dropped the buckeye coupling on the rear of the train and pulled out the buffers, ready for assistance. The 08 diesel duly arrived and towed us back to 'the gate', where we berthed the train and travelled home as passenger, making a bit of overtime into the bargain.

The second failure was not mine, but my train was used to assist. This was on Saturday, 5th November whilst working a Portsmouth – Victoria service, which had just been made up to a twelve-car formation at Barnham, 8CIG/4BEP. I was cautioned at Yapton AHB to pass a signal at danger and again at Ford home signal to come up behind a 4VEP unit standing at the platform. The driver was Biff Manvell from Horsham and his unit was a total failure, so it was arranged to couple on and propel to Littlehampton, Biff having charge of the brake. On arrival, we coupled off and I changed ends and got away, somewhat delayed but with clear signals, and started to make up a bit of time. I arrived at Victoria only six minutes after the departure of my return working, but that had been covered, so it was again home as passenger and a bit of overtime again.

The last episode was also a dead unit on the rear of the 10.20 Victoria to Brighton service one Saturday in August 1979, when the train was terminated at Selhurst with ECS into the depot and then continued empty to Gatwick Airport, with the remaining unit to pick up my return working to Victoria.

Non-EMU work was of course practically non-existent, but two jobs did occur, the first being on a Saturday in May 1978 when we were three drivers booked on at 04.00 to conduct track-maintenance machines from Horsham to Dorking, stabling them in the engineer's siding. I was away first at 04.30 and on arrival at Dorking we were all booked break and then as passenger back to Horsham, which was first possible at 09.38, that being the first train on a Saturday! We should have then rung the Foreman at Brighton but decided just to go home, after a vote of two to one, as we considered that there was not time enough to be given any further work.

The second occurrence was when sitting spare at the depot (14.25 booking on)one Sunday when I received a message to conduct a Brighton driver to Selhurst depot via Dorking, Sutton and West Croydon at 19.15. When the train arrived, it was a mixed traction driver with three DEMU sets, which gave a bit of variety, albeit a noisy one, and which he allowed me to drive. They had been in use on the west coastline because of electrical sub-station work.

There were some characters on our shift but on the whole a group of drivers who were prepared to help when needed. When our daughter was born, I was on the late shift getting back to the depot, too late to get to the hospital at Crawley for visiting hours, but several days that week, Eddie Jones, who was sitting spare, came up and relieved me at Crawley, thus enabling me to visit my wife and newborn child. One colleague could be easily flustered and was an easy one to windup, and if booking on spare we would sometimes say that the Foreman had been ringing after him and instantly a sweat would breakout, and throwing his bag on the table, Dave would get hold of the telephone without even removing his crash helmet. He was also often to be seen picking blackberries when in season, and we would make the same joke with him on returning and he always fell for it.

We had a period of one-day strikes one winter when there were severe frosts. We were on strike every second day, which meant that the days we were working the de-icing trains had not been out the previous night, so there was chaos on the following mornings. On the first morning, it was announced that we should try to start up the service towards Three Bridges and it was our aforementioned colleague whose train was to depart first. It was a single 4Vep unit, which after some rather severe arcing duly expired just outside the signalbox. After a long wait, a mixed traction driver turned up to

41

startup the 08 diesel shunter in the goods yard so that the unit could be rescued. Needless to say, nothing else moved that day!

One Sunday afternoon, I booked on for a turn that had been drastically altered as a result of engineering works south of the station, and only platform 4 was available. On booking on, there were no trains in sight, and because of bad planning the service had fallen completely apart, with nothing moving. It was a warm sunny day so all the windows and the door of the mess room were open, and one of our colleagues, who had a rather penetrating voice, was ranting on about the incompetence of management when suddenly an elderly woman knocked on the door and asked if the language could be moderated, whereupon 'Plum' replied that if she stood there any longer then she would hear a fxxxing sight more – he was not one for diplomacy, and said woman beat a hasty retreat!

Another day, when the morning rush hour had just about collapsed, there was total chaos at East Croydon where a senior railwayman on asking a guard what the trouble was introduced himself as the Divisional Movements Manager, to which the guard replied that if it was himself then he would probably keep quiet about that.

An interesting episode one late evening occurred when working the 22.36 from Victoria. Because of signal problems I had a sixteen-minute late start and on arrival at Horsham there was a large group of passengers on the platform, which was a bit unusual at this time of night, but it transpired that the last southbound service, 22.02 ex-Victoria, had been cancelled and the following terminating service had gone to the sidings. I was asked along with my guard if we were prepared to run a special as far as necessary to get the customers home, to which we agreed, the guard making a list of stops to make, and then we set off. In the end, we reached Chichester, where the last couple of passengers got a taxi to their final destination. It was a bit of an experience as all the station lights had been switched off and exit gates locked up. At Arundel, for example, we had to guide our passengers over the footbridge to the up-side platform and then help them climb over the iron railings. One man had thrown his briefcase over the fence, when one of the others promptly climbed up and jumped down, landing neatly on said case, completely crushing it.

British Railways Southern Region

Essex House
College Road
Croydon CR9 1NY
Tel 01-686 3422 Extn.   D. C. R. Mackmurdie Divisional Manager Central Division

Driver A.Evans.
E.M.U.T.
Horsham.

y/r
o/r

MP/DR. 3277.
3.11.77.

2236:Victoria to Horsham. 13.10.77.

A letter of appreciation has been received
from T.J.Rooth Esq,wishing on behalf of 40 or so
passengers and himself to thankyou for forward-
ing the above service,stopping intermediate
stations to Chichester. 2202.ex Victoria being
cancelled.

I wish to add my own thanks for your effort
in ensuring passengers arriving at the various
stations between Horsham and Chichester.

A copy of this letter will be attached to your
Staff Records.

DIVISIONAL MANAGER

L. AUSTIN
MOTIVE POWER ASSISTANT

Thank you letter for extra service 13/10/77

43

'Sorry about that, old boy,' he said, whereupon the reply was something like 'Oh, that's quite all right,' but one could hear between the lines, 'Stupid git!'

We returned ECS to Horsham and, after berthing the stock, had made three hours' overtime, which was later followed up by a letter of thanks from the Motive Power Officer on behalf of the customers. When the driver of the 22.06 from Victoria heard about it, he was a bit put out that it was not him that made the overtime. With regards to overtime, it was easy to make a quick buck with the 23.36 from Victoria as we were booked on arrival to shunt to the branch sidings and attach to a previously berthed unit. Officially, that meant preparing said unit before the attachment could be made, a provision not made for in the diagram, thus giving overtime each night. In reality, we just coupled on without 'cutting in' the second unit, giving a bit of easy money!

Apart from a fatality, which I will not go into, then the most dramatic day whilst at Horsham was on Monday, 20th March 1978. I had booked on at 05.30 to work the 06.13 service to Victoria via Dorking with 4SUB units 4285 and 4753.It was a dark and windy morning and having just passed Holmwood's colour light distant signal, I observed a tree laying across both tracks at cab height, resting on both banks. I dropped the 'deadman' and jumped to the offside of the cab.Luckily, I had been driving standing up; there was a loud bang and an electrical arc across the cab as the controller was pushed to the back of the cab, which would probably have inflicted considerable injuries if I had been sitting. I was a bit dazed but scrambled out of the cab with handlamp and detonators as the first down service was soon due. I managed to stop him and we were able to remove the remains of the tree so that he could continue towards Horsham. My guard had gone back to protect the rear of the train but instead of continuing to Ockley to use the telephone, he had returned, so he had to walk once again. It was no use going forward to Holmwood as the signalbox was not in general use at this time. An assisting train arrived at 08.05, consisting of two 4SUB units (originally 06.33 ex-Horsham) with Biff Manvell driving. We got coupled up, and with him driving and me braking, we got away ten minutes later. We stopped to pick up stranded passengers at Holmwood, who looked rather startled on seeing the front of the train as the front window was smashed and the whole cab front was crumpled in. On arrival at Dorking at 08.45, I was relieved from duty and made my way home, having the rest of the week off as I had hurt my hand when landing on the cab floor. On returning to work, I was looked up by a Motive Power Inspector who asked why I had not mentioned using track circuit clips in my report. According to the rules, I should have used them, but I pointed out that the accident occurred in a non-track circuit block area and also that Holmwood signalbox was switched out as normal, so who would see that there were set clips down? He got a bit upset about that but had to concede that it would have made no difference but only wasted time in stopping the approaching train.

The winter of 1981/82 gave us a sudden snowstorm, and after having completed the first half of my duty, a return trip to Victoria, the second half was cancelled because of the weather conditions. However, the Station Inspector asked me if I was willing to take a train to Victoria via Dorking as there had been no service on that route for several hours. I agreed, after fetching extra clothing and boots from home, if I could take an 8SUB formation as they had heavier shoe beams and one could cut out the leading shoes and use them as scrapers, thus saving shoe fuses. The trip went well, making reasonable time and then returning the same way. Mick Hockley from Horsham rode home as passenger with me in the cab, which proved to be useful as on the incline up to Sutton station I hit a low-hanging branch, resulting in me not being able to see out of my window, so Mick guided me into the station, where we could remove the snow. If I had been alone, I would have needed to stop, and there might have been some difficulties in starting again.

One morning when there was neither sickness nor holidays, we had a mess room full of spare men, with me being the first man on (05.30) after the cover man. The Brighton Foreman rang and sent the cover man home and said that I could take a route refresher. At that time, I had not long finished all my route learning, so where to go? I decided on Fratton carriage depot, which was somewhere we never came, so a day off! Lo and behold, the following Sunday, I was booked a special working which entailed travelling passenger to Fratton and collecting stock from the depot going ECS to Portsmouth Harbour. Well, I got there, and it was easy enough to get out of the depot, fortunately. The train was a 12VEP formation and was a return school excursion to New Cross Gate, which I was to work to Horsham, being relieved by a London Bridge driver. It was a non-stop run and the only time when I was signalled on the through line at Havant; something that is not possible today, the through lines having been removed.

In 1982, we had a two-week strike in connection with the management's intention of abolishing the eight-hour day and introducing flexible rostering. We were nearly 100% on strike, with just a few going into work, with consequent hard times afterwards. We returned to work after being threatened with the sack and no backup from the TUC. The last point was a foretaste of what was to come with the miners' strike in 1984/85, when the TUC again failed to deliver. So much for solidarity between unions, although there was always support between ASLEF and NUM.

At this time, I had already planned that I would be leaving the railway as my wife was not happy with living in England, which had got worse after the birth of our daughter. We were not happy with the Thatcher regime and did not want our daughter to go to school with God, Queen and Country, the rhetoric not getting any better with the Falklands War. There were also general cutbacks in the health service, plus the government's campaign against the unions. So, we put our house up for sale, which went rather more quickly than anticipated, and I resigned from British Rail ready for the move to Denmark. My last driving day was 14th October, an early turn finishing with a train via Dorking (4EPB 5020). The next day, I had to go to Redhill to the Area Depot Manager to hand in my keys, handlamp, etc. I rode up with Biff Manvell, being allowed to drive to Redhill (4CIG 7323), and that was the end of my first railway career. Some farewell parties followed, the removal folk came and emptied the house for shipment and then we set sail with DFDS from Harwich to start a new life, which I have never regretted. Thus ended eleven years with British Rail.

Last day in British Rail employment, Horsham 15/10/82

A Break from the Railways

I knew that a job on the railways in Denmark would be out of the question for the foreseeable future, alone because of the language barrier. I had also made some tentative enquiries and found that employment with the state railways carried civil service status, which required Danish citizenship, a process that could take up to seven years. So, what to do? A visit to the job centre revealed that I only had to have three months' employment to be entitled to unemployment benefit as I was given merit for having had employment and union membership in the UK, an advantage of both countries being in the European market! Not so easy today after the Brexit farce.

The job centre helped me to get a job with a photographer who was involved in restoring glass plates for the local history archives, and when that ended, I was unemployed for about eighteen months, which gave me ample time to take evening classes and get to grips with the language. I had the idea that now I had moved permanently to a new country then it was my duty to learn the language, so I forced myself to go out and about where I had to use it. For my first birthday in Denmark, my in-laws gave me membership of the Danish Railway Club and I made contact with a local branch that had a base at a small engine shed where restoration of a steam locomotive was in progress, plus maintenance of one other locomotive and some carriages. There was a working day each Tuesday evening and all day Saturday. This introduced me to a lot of technical words, which helped to broaden my vocabulary. There were no museum railways in our area so when out and about with our train then it was either on the local private railways, of which there were two, or else on the DSB main lines, being worked by our own personnel with a conductor driver, who generally offered their services in their free time.

I had to stop after finding employment as we now had two
children, and with us both now working full time, it was not easy to
fit it in. My first job was a short-term one helping my brother-in-law,
who was a carpenter, to renovate a factory roof, and then I landed a
job producing gravestones, which were turned out by the lorryload,
the granite coming in large blocks from Sweden and then being cut
out into large slices and then going through various processes before
going for export to West Germany and Holland. Although fairly well
paid, it was hard work and monotonous. All the time I was improving my language skills, and the time eventually came when I could
apply for citizenship. This was towards the end of 1988 and was a lot
easier then than it is today. There were a lot of forms to fill out and
documentation to be collected from England, and I had to have an
interview with a policeman attached to immigration so that he could
hear that I could speak Danish!

After waiting some months, I then received a fine document stating
that I was now a Danish citizen and that I had relinquished my
British citizenship. So, now I could get writing to DSB to seek
employment with them. The next hurdle was that as I had no educa-
tion within the metal industry, for example, mechanic, machine
worker, etc., then I could not be a train driver. *Pis*! So what were the
options? I wanted nothing to do with being a guard as I had no wish
to be on the receiving end of disgruntled passengers, but I found a job
that covered all manner of practical station work such as shunting,
carriage and wagon inspection, goods shed duties, etc., etc. I duly
applied and was invited to an admissions exam at Slagelse station on
a Saturday at the end of April 1989 after passing a medical. I think
that there were about a dozen of us attending, and we were informed
that there were vacancies at Ringsted, Slagelse and Kalundborg. I put
my name down for the latter, which was the easiest to get to and
from for me. The tests were quite comprehensive and took several
hours, with a break for lunch. We were then subjected to individual
interviews, where earlier in the day we had been informed that we
would not know the results of the tests until some days later.
However, during my interview, I was asked when I could start, which
came as a bit of a surprise. I was also told that as there were three

others who had also requested Kalundborg, they were prepared to start me in Holbæk, which was perfect, being just six kilometres from home. It just remained for me to be measured up for uniform, to be ordered from an extensive range of clothing. I had to give one month's notice to my employer and was thus able to begin with DSB on 1st June, the start of a thirty-year career.

DSB Groundstaff

Now came the day when my new railway career began at Holbæk station, where I would meet my local instructor at 08.00. Although we were at the end of the 1980s, there was still quite some activity there. Under the Station Manager were a Yard Foreman and twelve groundstaff, plus about the same number in the ticket office/travel bureau and five to cover signalling. There was no separate signalbox, the signalling panel being situated at the back of the ticket office, covering just the station as Roskilde controlled from one side and Kalundborg from the other. The permanent way department had a gang of four to five, and DSB also had a large bus depot in the town which covered all the town services, plus several out of town, so one can say that it had a significant presence in Holbæk.

Arriving at the station with some trepidation and wondering what I had let myself in for, I met my instructor, Svend, who immediately made me welcome and put me at my ease. One of the other staff asked him if he had come to work on his Harley that day, which I thought was rather impressive as he was not a very big man to have such a large machine, but it turned out to be an internal joke as his transport was a rather ancient moped! After a coffee, he took me to meet the Station Manager and then showed me around the station. It was a modern station, having been completely rebuilt in 1974, with three through platforms and two bays and the freight area comprising three sidings formed as loops and five dead-end sidings, plus a line down through the town to the harbour, which was used each weekday. There was quite a steep gradient down to the harbour and on arrival the tracks were dealt into two sections known as the old and new harbours, both of which had two long sidings with run-round facilities. Back at the station on the opposite side from the

51

main building were situated four carriage sidings with facilities for electric pre-heating of stock (1500v), watering and compressed air. On the Roskilde side there was a very long headshunt with a shorter one at the opposite end. The private railways (OHJ and HTJ) also had their main workshop/depot here, complete with active turntable, where our own shunting tractor was housed overnight. This was an 0-4-0DM built by Krupp Ardelt in the 1950s, later replaced by a 4wDH of '*køff*' type built in the 1960s by Frichs in Aarhus, which was a copy of the German '*kleinloks*'.

The work at Holbæk was varied, with both passenger and goods trains being attended to, plus helping as required with shunting for the private railway's loco-hauled services. We had three rakes of passenger stock (push-and-pull sets), one of eight carriages and two each of five berthed overnight, and the overnight goods train from København usually deposited between fifteen and twenty wagons each morning. There were also some fixed jobs that had to be done each week. On Wednesdays, we had to wash down the subway and associated stairs up to the platforms with a high-pressure hose, and on Thursdays, we had oiling of all the power points doing the east and west ends of the station on alternate weeks. At other times, the hand points would be oiled, plus the platform lines kept free of rubbish.

Freight traffic was mostly incoming, with quite a variety of goods such as sawn timber, grain, animal feed, fertiliser, copper wire, wine in tank wagons, frozen foods in Interfrigo vans, used cars from Germany, plus some military traffic, and in the spring we would receive up to forty vans loaded with charcoal from Yugoslavia (for the grill season). Every Monday, we received a van of egg boxes from a packaging factory destined for a local packing station. Outgoing traffic could be paper for recycling, felled trees and scrap metal, so a large variety of freight wagons would be seen. A close eye had to be kept on the loading, especially of scrap, as the truck drivers tried to load according to volume and not weight. Any traffic for the permanent way department would also be conveyed in the ordinary freight trains. In the summer, there would be a goods van included for the transport of cycles sent in advance, which was still big business at this time.

To be employed as a civil servant, the first two years was a trial period when one's local manager had to periodically assess one's progress. Apart from my local instructor, I was also allocated an instructor to whom I had to report once a month together with the three new recruits in Kalundborg, where we were instructed in rules and signalling, railway geography in Denmark and technical instruction for carriages and wagons. At that time, DSB was a large concern which as well as rail services also had a bus division and a shipping division. From Kalundborg there were two ferry services to both Aarhus and the island of Samsø, so sometimes our tuition was at sea. Several examinations had to be passed along the way, the first being a shunting exam and then after about six months of employment I had to attend the railway school in København for one month, which culminated in several exams allowing one to work independently. About this time, the station was supplied with a *køff* shunting tractor, and it was decreed that we all had to gain a licence to drive so that we could be used more flexibly, there being only three or four of the older shunters who were proficient to drive the previous tractor.

Most of the shifts were early turns, with just one man on duty on late and night turns and at weekends, and we covered the whole week except Saturday nights between 01.30 and 05.30. The night shift could be classed as the hardest. Starting at 22.30, there would be two rakes of passenger stock berthed of which one would have been seen after by the late turn man, so the first job was to fill the water tanks and make both an external and internal inspection of the second rake, which comprised eight carriages, this also including any small repairs required or writing in the repair book for anything else. It would then be time to go over to the platforms and receive the third train to be berthed and after getting the all-clear from the guard that it was empty, we would arrange to shunt the train using two-way radio. On berthing the train, the locomotive would remain coupled but with the brake pipe cocks between locomotive and carriages closed – this being a precaution so that when the locomotive was prepared next morning, it would not be possible for the train to accidently run away, which would be detrimental to the air pipe and pre-heat cable attached. Heating of locomotive-hauled stock in Denmark is at 1500v, 800A, and we attached external air supply so that we could test the working of toilets and doors when examining the stock.

One night, the shunter on duty had forgotten to close the brake pipes and the preparing driver had let the train roll just a couple of metres, but that was enough to pull the heating cable out whilst pre-heating at full power, which resulted in all the paintwork being burnt off the corner of the carriage, plus a meltdown of the cable and socket! The cables always had to be handled with respect and with appropriate precautions. Back to the night turn, this last train would also be examined and watered and then it would be time for the arrival of the morning goods train from København, when we would meet the driver and receive the relevant paperwork before going to the rear of the train to uncouple the wagons for us and move the tail lamps to the wagon now in rear for Kalundborg. The last job was to prepare the first two departures for København at 05.06 and 05.36, which involved a full brake test, checking that all vehicles could brake and release, and then shunting them to the platform. The driver would drive from the driving trailer carriage, and the shunter would stand on the shunter's step on the locomotive, just great in rain or snow! The duty finished at 06.30 after a night that included walking about ten kilometres.

The day shifts were mostly concerned with goods traffic, passenger shunting finishing around 08.00. The incoming wagons would be sorted and around 08.30 we would proceed to the harbour, much to the chagrin of many motorists having to wait for us to pass as we could control the various sets of traffic lights on our way! On arrival, there was the possibility of running round the wagons, but the older shunters preferred to stop on the bank before the harbour, uncouple the tractor and draw it forward to a siding and then take the wagons by on the handbrake before coupling the tractor on the rear – all to save five minutes. Everything normally proceeded okay, but occasionally it would go wrong, and then it was all hands to the pump to stop the wagons before crossing the next road, which was often busy with lorries to and from the quayside. That really got the adrenalin flowing, but they would do the same again the next day!

We often received flat wagons with timber for the local building merchants, which would be covered with tarpaulins. These would have to be folded, roped and sent return. One morning, I was together with a very big-built colleague who showed me what to do, having four such wagons that day. Having folded and roped the first, he said that I should just throw it up onto the wagon, which I tried but could hardly get it up off the ground! It was the same with lifting the sides up on an open wagon; he could do it with one hand where I would be struggling. When receiving open wagons for loading, the Yard Foreman would insist on them being swept out, which could be a filthy job and a job that was obviously not done at all stations as some of the wagons could yield several barrowloads of rubbish. Fish-meal would also be received in paper sacks, and sometimes they were not loaded properly so that there was some spillage, these also having to be swept out. It was fortunate that we had good shower facilities.

We would also assist with shunting the few loco-hauled trains run by the private railway. Each morning, the school train would arrive, comprising an ex-DSB class Mx diesel with four carriages which we would shunt over to the carriage sidings, and if the 'wrong' depot staff were on duty then all the carriages would have to be split up and rearranged. Occasional freight trains would also be run for which we would be responsible for assisting with brake testing. In the summer period, loco-hauled services would be run to cope with the extra traffic to 'summerland', and on Sundays two through services to København. The carriages were a mixture of ex-DSB, new build from the 1960s and from a defunct German tour agency. These we would assist with running the locomotives round the stock. One interesting point with the private railway stock was that each carriage had its own oil-fired heating system as opposed to receiving it from the loco-motive.

One Sunday afternoon whilst still with my instructor, Svend, the train from the private railway was running late and arrived about ten minutes after the train to København had departed. It was high summer and there were a lot of passengers returning from the beaches and summer houses who were a little irate, which did not get any better when, on approaching us, they asked Svend when the next departure would be. He looked quietly at them and, sucking on his pipe, said that it would be already in one hour. They looked at him in disbelief, being used to a much more intensive service in the capital but luckily did not become more enraged.

The rush-hour terminating trains could also have some interest, often just lost items of luggage which the guard had missed, but one afternoon one of the toilets was still occupied when after banging on the door a bedraggled pair emerged, rather red in the face, especially when they found out that they had travelled on the wrong train and were many miles away from their destination! The sequel to this was that on berthing the stock, I was called up on the radio to inspect the toilet to look for missing contact lenses. They did not turn up!

Train failures could also occur as on one afternoon when two rush-hour trains arrived coupled together, with the foremost locomotive a complete failure, so I had on platform two – the station's longest – a train comprising two locomotives and sixteen carriages, with only one active locomotive in the middle. That took a bit of sorting out, berthing one rake of stock and removing two carriages from the second as normal practice, before returning it to service, with the dead locomotive coupled inside the good one.

In the beginning of the '90s, the local council purchased four redundant carriages from DSB and converted them into a youth hostel as a project for young unemployed. When the project was complete, there was held an opening day, a Saturday, the council requesting that there should be run three trips from the station to the harbour and return to show off the results, and this was in connection with the Danish Railway Club. A diesel locomotive and driver were borrowed from the private railway, and I would be leading shunter for the day. It all went off successfully, and the stock was to be berthed in the goods yard again. On approaching the buffer stops, all the yard lighting went out and I quickly stopped the driver before calling up the signalling panel saying that we had been very close to demolishing the buffer stops, the response being silence for a few moments. The man on duty had a habit of turning off most of the station lighting between trains, thinking that he was saving electricity, and he had momentarily forgotten that we were shunting in the yard. I think that there was probably more wear and tear on the strip lighting than actual savings. Many apologies, and then we could continue with our work.

Some of the older staff seemed to think that they were experts in sorting out the various goods wagons and would sometimes ask why I did not do this and that as they would have done, so one day, after sorting about twenty wagons and having received such a comment, I sat down with a piece of paper and asked how they would have done it, setting it down on paper and then writing down how I had arranged the shunting. There was exactly the same number of movements but no comments!

If there was not anybody on holiday or sick then the Yard Foreman had to find work for us not on the fixed roster. This was not always that easy, and sometimes we would be sent out on loan to other stations, which could be good financially as if the conditions were right (a longer period) then one was paid an extra month's pay tax-free, but usually it was just odd days but still receiving a tax-free supplement. I had been to Kalundborg to be trained on the station layout and the daily routines so was often called upon to help out there. One afternoon shift entailed working out on the main line to a private siding (Avnsøgaard), serving a quarry that serviced DSB with ballast, and the first time that I had this job alone, on returning to Kalundborg, the Yard Foreman asked me for the freight despatches. I looked at him, not understanding what he meant but soon getting the gist of it when he started ranting on about emptying a letterbox at the sidings, a job that my instructor had omitted to tell me about, so now it was his turn to get an earful as he happened to be on duty that day. I made sure that I had all the paperwork with me next time.

Kalundborg was a busy station at that time with a lot of freight, plus a workshop for passenger stock and a locomotive depot. Part of my training also involved being out-stationed at the parcels terminal in Ringsted for a whole month when DSB employed a large fleet of road vehicles for collection and distribution. There were two shifts involved, 11-19 and 22-06. The 'day' shift would receive the incoming trucks, sorting of goods and then loading into rail wagons. The night shift would be the reverse, except that the lorry drivers loaded their own vehicles according to their own requirements.

The private siding at Avnsøgaard was also used to deposit used ballast, and that gave me three months' work, booking on at 05.00 each weekday and travelling on the locomotive to Svebølle, where we ran round the train and then worked up to the siding. To get in and out of the siding, there was an electronic release from the Kalundborg signalling panel so that one could remove the key to open the siding, closing it again once the train was inside. There was quite a steep incline within the siding, which could be a bit of a challenge depending on the class of locomotive allocated to the job. At first, it was with two class Mx but later an Mz, which was okay, but on odd days it was an Me, which on a damp rail struggled quite a bit. After emptying the hoppers, it was then time to get permission to leave the siding for the return, where I would drop off at Holbæk, which was generally about 11.00 as the drivers were eager to get away as soon as possible. The Yard Foreman looked down his nose a bit at me finishing early each day, but he did not say anything and I did not, either. The Foreman also got a bit upset one day when on arriving for work he could not see the shunting tractor in the yard. It was a slack period for freight traffic and we had decided that as there was no incoming traffic and nothing to collect at the harbour then it was a waste of time starting it up and bringing it out! We were made aware that it was not up to us to decide and that we should immediately fetch it out, which we did, parking it in the yard and then returning it at the end of the shift! The Foreman was of the old-school type, which we could also see when he was preparing the paperwork for the outgoing wagons. He was not altogether sure about the EDB system that was in use, so instead of just going around the wagons using the hand terminal, he would also note the information on paper 'just in case'!

After being employed 'on trial' for two years and providing one had passed the necessary exams and one's conduct was deemed satisfactory, one became permanently employed, which was a big day as one received two months' pay. This was because for the first two years one was paid in arrears and as a civil servant in advance.

Seniority included the two trial years. So, double pay on 1st June 1991, just in time for the summer holidays. On being permanently employed, I could now begin to study the 'escape' list, which came out each month with vacancies throughout DSB. Easier said than done as seniority was always the most important factor, so I filled out many applications before it was my turn, which came along in the spring of 1993 when I filled a vacancy in København at the Helgoland carriage depot, which meant no more freight work.

Helgoland was divided into two parts, with the carriage sidings and washing plant situated between the coastlines to/from Helsingør and a large workshop situated on the opposite side of the outward-going coastline reached by an underpass. The coastline came under the panelbox at København H, but the depot itself had its own signalbox as when shunting at the west end of the depot we often had to go out onto the main line, there being only a very short headshunt. There was also a headshunt at the east end of the yard, so most of the sidings were double-ended, which made the workings very flexible. This was the main depot for locomotive-hauled stock as, although the regional stock of type Bn/ABns was nominally allocated to both Kalundborg and Nykøbing F, some work was also carried out here, together with IC stock and night stock. The night trains were internal Danish services and comprised ex-DB couchette carriages and hired British Rail Mk3 sleepers, plus seasonal services to Austria for skiing/summer holidays which were made up of DSB couchettes. There were also berthed three sets of DB stock overnight for services to Hamburg, and we supplied stock to all manner of special services including three German-built saloon carriages that could be hired for conferences, etc. These three vehicles still exist, one as a measuring vehicle and the other two as the royal train. Shunting power was a class Mh(similar to a DB V60) on a weekday day shift and a *køff* tractor, plus main line locomotives were used when required. Staffing consisted of a Yard Master on a day shift and Yard Foremen, plus shunters round the clock. During the day, many trains came into the yard to reverse before returning westwards and would either go through the washer or have alterations to their formation, sometimes both. Many of the staff were of a younger generation, and coupled with the fact that there is a difference in attitude between people from the country and from large cities it was a bit of a culture shock to come here. There was not so much thought about helping colleagues to make the day go easier,so it was very much each man for himself.

In the middle of the '90s, it was decided to close the workshops at Kalundborg and Nykøbing F and concentrate all carriage mainten- ance at Helgoland. The carriage sidings at Østerport, which had previously only been used for three to four rakes of stock between rush hours, would now be putto full use as an out-station to Helgo- land, with the *køff* tractor being moved there and Helgoland acquiring a second Mh for three shifts, seven days a week. There was to be more staff allocated to Østerport, and I volunteered to go there, it being a bit easier to travel to/from home. There was a fan of nine carriage sidings of various lengths which were full up both at night and between rush hours, and they were manned 24/7.Being much smaller than Helgoland, there was a lot more of giving each other a helping hand and as it was a long station,to save a lot of walking when there were two on duty, we would split up so that when sending trains out in service, one would do all the brake testing and then the other could call the trains back to the outlet roads. One had to keep oneself alert at all times as between the carriage sidings and staff block were situated tracks that connected a small marshalling area with Frihavn, where the train ferry from Helsingborg in Sweden docked, transporting freight wagons, and there would be nearly constant shunting to and fro.

I think that it was about 1995 when DSB decided to try a motorail service to Austria for the summer period using DSB couchette carriages and hired DB double-deck car carriers. A disused loading ramp was refurbished and the trains departed on Friday evening, returning Sunday afternoon, which gave a bit of extra work as we carried out the shunting with our *køff*, which was not normally used on the late turn or at the weekends. I was on duty the first Sunday and on arrival the car owners were met by customs officers (this was before the Schengen Agreement), and it was amusing to see their faces as it was several hours since they had passed the

German/Danish border, some of them not looking too happy with the situation. Too much wine and spirits in the car maybe? Østerport was used mainly for the berthing of regional train formations at night and between rush hours, plus some inter-regional services that used the train ferry from Korsør to Nyborg before the building of the bridge over the Storebælt. That got me a reprimand one day as when brake testing for a departure the leading carriage would not release the brake so, as per regulations, I pulled the release cord and isolated the brake. However, I had forgotten that on arrival at Nyborg the ferry would do an about-turn before entering the harbour, meaning that the carriage with the isolated brake would now be on the rear of the train! Not so good as either the train would have to be remarshalled or an extra carriage found to add to the rear. Never made that mistake again!

Isolating brakes was a common occurrence for a variety of reasons, the most common being worn or cracked brake blocks. This of course meant a reduction in brake force, and if it was a short formation then it could affect timekeeping as a result of a reduction in the speed allowed. One winter, we experienced a night with many frost degrees and a good layer of snow when control had requested that at about 02.00 we should have a ten-carriage set pulled out ready to be collected by a locomotive, which should be on its way, so we coupled on our *køff* to pump up air and then proceeded to try and free the brake blocks, which were frozen to the wheels with an iron bar. Having accomplished that, we couldn't pull the stock out as it was frozen to the rails! At the same time, control called to say that this special working was now cancelled, which did not help our frame of mind. Lars, whom I was working with that night, had dropped his keys by a set of hand points and did not find them again for several weeks until the snow had melted.

One very interesting train we received was in August 1995, which arrived from Amersfoort in Holland as empty stock, comprising nine vehicles from the former East German state train. This was a charter train for, I believe, young students. We also dealt with special trains for football fans and for school summer camps. These were always made up of ten former intercity compartment carriages, which had to be fitted with destination boards and reservation labels, which took a considerable time over and above our normal duties.

About this time, there was a raid at Helgoland where there was uncovered an illicit alcohol dive in the machine house above the carriage washer, where a ledger with names and transactions recorded was found! As a result, three Yard Foremen were removed from their posts and a couple of shunters fired. There was obviously an acute staffing problem, which was resolved firstly by two Foremen transferring in from another yard and the third place being offered to me on a temporary basis by our Depot Manager as a trial. I had previously been to a manager/staff interview when I had expressed my interest in promotion, and as DSB had at long last altered promotions so that it was not just seniority that counted but also whether one was suitable for the position, my chance had now come, and after the trial period I was appointed Yard Foreman from 1st August 1996, with a considerable rise in salary.

Helgoland was exceptionally busy at this time and the two Mh shunters were fully occupied, which also included trips to Østerport to swap carriages to/from maintenance. Also at this time the carriage controllers moved out to Helgoland, which made life a little easier as one could go over to their office to discuss problems without having to hang on the telephone all the time. The day shift could be especially strenuous, with both Mh at work and carriages being called in for maintenance and being released for traffic, so there was constant shunting. The first job in the morning was to make out a work list for the shunters and then it was just to follow on with the day's programme. Friday was the worst day as more trains were run up to the weekend, plus many of the normal services also had to be increased in size. If I remember correctly, I needed thirty-eight extra carriages to be used from about mid-morning onwards, and sometimes when arriving at 07.00, the yard would be almost completely empty, so you knew that it would be one of those days when you would be robbing carriages from here, there and everywhere. All types could suddenly be used, totally ignoring the marshalling plans, except on the coastline to Helsingør, where it was a sin to send IC carriages instead of Bn material as too much time would be lost at stations as IC stock had fewer doors. The weekend would then be used to clear up the mess, but I did pride myself on the fact that I did not have a day when we didn't get all trains away on time and with the right number of carriages. We had one extra-long siding, track 8, where all spare carriages would be congregated and one morning it was completely full, with sixteen vehicles, and right in the middle was a particular carriage that had to be dug out for later use, so the shunter got his list of where all sixteen carriages were to be used and off he went. After about three hours' continuous shunting, they came in for a break but whilst out writing up the yard, I saw that in the middle of track 8 was the same carriage that had been there earlier, so on entering the mess room I mentioned it to the shunter, who then had to tell the Mh driver that they had to go out and start again, which was not met with much enthusiasm.

I did not experience many problems with the staff as if one has the right attitude then one can get all the work done without complaint. One Friday, however, we had a shunter on loan from København and instead of following my request, he planted an incoming ECS in the washing track but without bringing it in far enough, so it was still foul of the other tracks in the rear. When I asked him what he was doing, as the yard was completely full and nothing could move, he just flipped out, threw his radio over two tracks, smashing it in the process, and stalked off, saying he was going home. I couldn't ignore that, so after sorting out the chaos, I had to report him to the Yard Master, and I believe that it resulted in the radio having to be paid for.

Each year, there would be held a planning conference before implementation of the new timetable to optimise staff usage. In 1997, it was my turn to attend, together with representatives from all the depots in eastern Denmark. We started off with a clean whiteboard which was divided up into twenty-four hours and seven days, and then we would mark up each train that came to the depot with details of what had to be done with them and how much time was to be used, and that way we could see how many staff had to be on duty at any given time. Our Depot Manager was also present. He had now become manager for all the depot stations in our area, and I asked

him if we should make allowances for untoward episodes as Helgoland was responsible for all carriage maintenance, to which he
answered that it was DSB's philosophy that all trains ran to time and
that there were no faults with them! Results? Yes, not always somebody to take on an extra task. As the conference was over two days,
it was held at a bit of a posh hotel, which caused a bit of amusement
when we were to eat dinner. The food was served, what there was of
it, and one of the delegates called the waiter and asked him to call for
a taxi so that he could be transported to the food in the middle of his
plate, which did not go down too well! There was a queue at the
local sausage bar afterwards to satisfy the inner man.

During 1997, the workload at Helgoland had been reduced with
the introduction of some electric multiple units, and there would be a
reduction in the number of Yard Foremen as we were not to be there
24/7 in the future, and so I was offered a post at Kalundborg, which
I jumped at, even though it was only afternoon and night shifts. At
the same time, there had been a change in criteria for becoming a
driver, and although I had not driven Mh shunters, had not been to
technical school and was also too old (I was now forty-four), my
colleagues dared me to apply, which I did. I was invited to an interview and an admission exam at about the same time as starting at
Kalundborg, much to my manager's disappointment, as he had
already arranged for me to attend a leadership course, which would
take the best part of a year, with five weeks away spread out through
the year. He took it very well, however, and I got my diploma, so now
at the end of the summer, 1997, it was goodbye to Helgoland and
away from the big city atmosphere.

But before leaving Helgoland, some incidents to be categorised as
Alan's follies. The first was when shunting an ABns driving trailer
carriage into the workshop building when after having opened the
roller shutter doors, the movement back was called, resulting in a
rending of metal as I had failed to observe that the door was not fully
open, and as the driving trailers had a high sitting cab there was the
inevitable damage.

The second concerned a more potential danger and occurred as
follows. On Sunday afternoons, there was an incoming train from

Næstved, which always had the locomotive leading. This was because it was diagrammed with a driving trailer converted to operate with both diesel and electric locomotives, and the drivers at Næstved had not yet been trained on them. On this day, it arrived in the washer track because its normal place was occupied, so when that became free we would have to propel back to the headshunt and then forward to its rightful place. The headshunt could accommodate a loco plus four carriages, which was just right for this train, so I contacted the signalbox and received permission to shunt, this being the Foreman's job as there had been a saving of one shunter position on the late turn. So, we began to propel the train and at a strategic point I jumped off, ready for the next move, but then the train stopped without me saying anything to the driver. I asked him why he had stopped and he replied that it had stopped by itself, so I then asked how many carriages there were and he replied five! Shit! I contacted the signalbox to stop all traffic on the main line and went to investigate. There were no buffer stops in the headshunt, just an earth and gravel bank, and the leading bogie was completely buried! Luckily, we were free of the main line, but all passing trains would be cautioned. I uncoupled the derailed carriage and shunted the rest of the train to the sidings whilst the signalman was alerting the breakdown train, which duly arrived to dig the carriage out. The driver of the train was Tommy Jørgensen from Næstved, more of whom later in this narrative. I was called to an interview with my manager the day after and I escaped with a warning as it was my first reported misdemeanour. Just two days later, I was moving a *køff* tractor, which derailed as a result of defective track, but just as it happened my manager walked by, stopping up to look and then looking at me. He just shook his head and walked on!

The shifts at Kalundborg were a result of DSB being split up into passenger and goods divisions, so apart from one shunter and the Yard Master on a day shift, all the passenger side activities were between 15.00 and 07.00, whilst the goods side had only early shifts. We were to be two Yard Foremen in two newly established positions that were previously covered by temporarily upgraded shunters, both myself and my opposite number being imported from elsewhere, which caused a bit of a stir in the beginning. One in particular could not understand how I could get the job as he had more seniority than me and had covered the job for quite some time. However, on saying that I was already appointed as Foreman and that I had taken the initiative to transfer to the København area and seek promotion, he then came to accept me.

We had two *køff* tractors for shunting, one standing spare as in case of a failure we were a long way from the nearest workshop. The facilities at Kalundborg comprised several carriage sidings, a washing plant and locomotive sidings, plus a fuelling point placed at the station between tracks two and three, close to the buffer stops. During the day, the carriage sidings were practically empty, apart from two carriages taken out of a train after the rush hour and put in again in the afternoon. At night, the situation was the complete opposite, with fifty-one carriages stabled, along with four MF (IC3) DMU sets and in the locomotive sidings seven class ME/MZ were stabled. To enable so much to be there overnight, we had full use of the goods loop to accommodate the first two departures, which being early could vacate the loop before the arrival of the goods train at 04.56. The station had its own signalling panel accommodated in the main station building and also controlled the line as far as Holbæk's home signal, with all stations but one having passing loops. The line was also single from Holbæk to Roskilde, apart from two short sections from Holbæk to Vipperød and Lejre to Roskilde, so the trains had to be precise as there could be many crossings, especially in peak periods. A signal failure or level-crossing barrier failure, of which there were many (signals and crossings, not failures), could cause havoc with the timetable, not to mention what a train failure could do.

I soon settled in, although it was a bit hard not having any day shifts, the rota being 23-07 Sunday to Thursday and 15-23 Monday to Friday, so the weekends were one short and one long, so time with the family had to be maximised as best as possible. The afternoon shift started with printing out all incoming trains and checking the formations and anything extra that might have to be done with them, also checking which outgoing services they were allocated to, thereafter deciding where they were to be berthed after servicing so that when the shunters booked on, they could see what I had planned. On arrival, all locomotives would be refuelled before propelling the stock to the sidings, normally the wash road, where they would be uncoupled and shunted to the loco sidings. The *køff* would then be coupled on and would shunt the stock first to toilet emptying/watering, which was situated within the washing plant building, and then through the washer and to berthing. This was done with all the trains staying overnight, with the staff being on the go all evening with a minimal break as we had a gentlemen's agreement that if they were finished when the night shift booked on, they could then go home about an hour early. All carriages also had to have a daily inspection and any small repairs carried out, so the night shift could also be busy as the last train did not arrive until 02.18 and the service started up again already at 04.16, so there was not a lot of spare time.

My time as Foreman at Kalundborg was only for about eighteen months and was generally uneventful. There was a spate of defective driving trailers where the defect was first discovered by the driver under preparation, which usually gave us a bit of a headache as the loco had to be coupled off and the carriages pulled to the platform by our tractor and the loco recoupled at the opposite end, the tractor being rescued after the departure. This of course gave extra work at a time of day when everybody had their own work to carry out, so it was up to the Foreman to give a hand. There was also a period when there had been several shunting collisions at both Kalundborg and Nykøbing F, resulting in quite a lot of damage. It was therefore decreed by management that as long as there was an active driving trailer in the formation then the driver should change ends each time there was a change of direction to eliminate as much propelling as possible. A circular was sent out to all drivers and all shunting staff, and this decision caused a lot of annoyance, especially amongst the drivers. During the first week of these new procedures, I met an incoming train at the buffer stops and said to the driver that he should tell me when he was ready at the other end, to which he replied that he had no intention of changing ends. No use arguing, so I informed him that he would then have to return with eight carriages instead of six and that the matter would have to be reported. I learnt later that he was a driver instructor and that he would now be just a plain driver, being deemed unsuitable to instruct.

The biggest event during these eighteen months was on 6th January 1998 when there was a head-on collision between two passenger trains at Regstrup, the last station before Holbæk. The train from Kalundborg was not booked to stop there but was booked to cross a service from København. On this morning, it was delayed and was waiting at the home signal when the driver of the train from Kalundborg misread his signals, colliding at about 30km/hr. Luckilyno loss of life, but considerable damage, with the driving trailer riding up the front of the ME locomotive and coming to a standstill at an acute angle. I was on night shift that week and on booking on, the station was empty, with nothing for us to do. However, at about 03.00, the first of two ECS workings arrived with two trains coupled together so that we had four trains ready to start the morning service with. They had been standing at Holbæk waiting to come through, and it took a bit of sorting out on arrival, having to leave one train on the main line whilst shunting the first to the sidings, the driver then retrieving the second and shunting that also and then repeating the process with the next arrival.

Towards the end of 1998, my time as Yard Foreman was running out and a new chapter in my career was to begin as a train driver once again. I could hardly wait!

Driving Again

We are now in the middle of December 1998 and preparations are being made for me to begin my training as a driver. It was arranged that I would be on loan to the motive power department for eight months until the training was completed, both the basic training plus the first traction course, which would be for GM diesel locomotives. This meant that I would retain my rate of pay as a Yard Foreman, which was higher than a Junior Driver's rate of pay, so until my seniority reached the same as a Senior Driver I would be somewhat better off than my peers! The depot at Kalundborg at this time was still situated within the former locomotive depot building with the usual facilities of booking-on point, locker room, mess room, toilets, etc. This building and the associated carriage workshop were now unstaffed for maintenance purposes, the locomotive building, though, still being used for the stabling of a main line loco on one track and shunting tractors on the other. Outside, there were stabling facilities (compressed air and battery charging) for five locomotives, and any other locomotives would be parked in front of their respective carriages if necessary.

My first day, 15th December, was for me to meet my group leader together with the local union representative and be shown around the depot and allocated a locker. I then received a rucksack filled with diverse literature (rule book, appendixes, etc.).The next day would be an introduction day out on the track with a driving instructor, and then it was arranged for me to have a week with a Locomotive Inspector for an intensive rules course with examination so that I could be on the same level as the other constituents on the course to which I was enrolled as they were already employed as drivers, either on a private railway or DSB's S-bane system.

This introduction day was an early turn (04.46), when I was to meet my instructor and follow his day's work. After booking on, we went out to find our locomotive, which was an MZ IV, where he proceeded to show me the preparation routine. This began with the removal of external air and electric connections and a visual inspection of the locomotive, making sure that all air pipes and couplings were hung up on their respective hooks, battery boxes locked, all brake blocks present and in good order and no apparent damage anywhere, plus control of the diesel tank gauge. The next step was to enter the locomotive and close the battery switch so that some lighting could be shed on the scene and then proceed to the start panel, which was situated at the compressor end of the engine. No such luxury as pressing a button on the cab desk; this was pure General Motors with all the accompanying noise! The priming pump was first started and then one could go round the engine room carrying out diverse checks before returning to start the engine, which meant turning the starter and at the same time giving the engine gas from a hand throttle until the engine fired, and also controlling oil pressure and coolant level. One could then turn a switch so that control was transferred from the engine room to the two cabs and then retire to quieter surroundings. Now both cabs had to be prepared with testing of brakes, driver's safety device, radio etc., etc. All this had to be completed within thirty minutes, which was rather daunting, but after a while routine set in, and this could be easily achieved so long as no problems arose.

So now the locomotive was ready and my instructor called up the shunter and we received permission to move out and be coupled to our train. This was a commuter train made up of ten carriages in push-pull formation, the locomotive pushing towards København. After being coupled on, we proceeded to the driving trailer carriage to prepare that, and then when ready the shunter would come to assist with a brake test, which was a lot different to that I had experienced in England. Firstly, the brake, after filling the train pipe, would be shut down to see if there were any leaks; the train pipe must not lose more than a half-kilo pressure in one minute, and if that was satisfactory then the system would be refilled and the brake would be applied by reducing the pressure by 0.65 kilo. The shunter would then check that all brake blocks were applied to the wheels, where-upon he would call for the brake to be released so that he could check that they were all loose again. This was known as an A-test and would be made every time that a train was to enter service for the first time. If at any time extra vehicles were added then the new vehicles would be tested, along with the next incoupled vehicle of the existing train, this being a B plus C-test. If vehicles were removed from the train then a C-test would be carried out when recoupling the locomotive to check that the train had been recoupled correctly. Lastly, there was a D-test, which would be carried out from the last vehicle in a train after the locomotive had been moved from one end to the other, a so-called run round. All this is still applicable to today's locomotive-hauled trains.

Now back to my first day. Preparation and brake testing were now complete with the result that the brake was isolated on one carriage and the electric dynamic brake on the locomotive was inoperative. My instructor propelled the train to the platform and then directed me to the hot seat. This particular departure, one hour and forty-five minutes after booking on, was a semi-fast train, and the first stop at Jyderup was a bit of a challenge as with ten carriages, the leading cab had to be placed practically under the platform starter signal or else the level- crossing barriers at the rear end would not go up and the starter could not be cleared! The Knorr braking system was a bit like the Westinghouse system I knew although it could be gradually released, one could quickly run short of air if one made two or three applications without giving the system time to recharge, so the braking method was the same, meaning a fairly high-speed approach, a heavy application releasing at the appropriate point to ensure stopping at the right mark with all brakes released. It sounds easy and generally is after some practice. This first day's work comprised working to Øster-port, where the train was berthed for the return rush-hour, and then travel as passenger back to København H, where after a break we worked back to Kalundborg.

Next was the rules course, where I was instructed to meet up with an Inspector at Korsør station, where we could work undisturbed. I had of course a knowledge of the rule book in my capacity as a shunter, but the next five days went much deeper and culminated with an oral exam on the fifth day, when there was a representative from the union to see fair play. After about ninety minutes, he declared that he did not need to hear anymore, and I was deemed fit to join the training course at the beginning of the new year. This was on 23rd December and then I had four days off for Christmas followed by three days out on the track and another four days off for New Year, with the course starting on Monday, 4th January at the DSB school at Østerport.

This basic course, known as LGU-S, was a newly revised course that was designed to simplify, for example, technical diagrams, meaning that one had to have an understanding of the diagrams without having to follow them in depth. This was achieved up to a point, but our Instructors were of the old school and many of the diagrams used had not been updated, so the course was a mix of old and new, which at times caused some confusion and discussion as often the new material had not arrived when starting a new theory module, forcing the Instructors to use the existing diagrams, which was also frustrating for them. The course alternated between theory and practical modules, eight of each, all practical periods being at one's home depot. The technical modules were as follows: diesel motor, transmission types, compressed air and braking systems, control systems, which included multiple coupling, push-and-pull operations and computer control, plus we had to have a general knowledge of carriage and wagon types and technicalities. The remaining modules dealt with rules and regulations and knowledge of employment conditions. There was a lot to learn and not much time to cover it, my biggest challenge being learning the Danish technical terms for the various components. We were a class of eighteen, all of whom, except myself, were already drivers, fifteen of them being destined for Helsingør depot, one for København and two of us for Kalundborg, and we had two Instructors.

The course was relatively concentrated, each theory module

ending with a short test and the Driving Instructor at the end of each practical period reporting back on progress via a log book, which we had to have with us at all times. At the end of the course, we were subjected to a series of tests that had to be passed before we were allowed to continue with the actual traction courses. Everybody managed to pass, although a couple had a bit of difficulty with the rules exam even though they had experience of driving. All those destined for Helsingør depot then received the information that they would not be trained on diesel locomotives as it had been decided that the depot would only have electric work in the foreseeable future, this being revoked at a later date. That meant that we would be only three to attend the diesel course and that would cover both class ME and MZ Series 4, plus two types of driving trailer carriages, one type as built for diesel operation and one type that had been converted to be able to run with either diesel or electric traction. The course was held at the Central Works and adjacent diesel depot in København, so it would be easy enough to go out and 'borrow' a locomotive as needed. Funnily enough, we had the same two Instructors again and as we were so few, we were able to go into much more detail.

This course finished with a written exam where I achieved 98% correct answers. We were now ready to take the practical exam and in due course I received notification that on 10th August I should report to the Instructors' office at København H. Meeting up with two examiners, we proceeded down to the platforms to relieve on a train that was comprised of ten carriages with a class MZ on the rear, which I had to drive to Østerport, where on arrival the train had to be shunted and berthed in the carriage sidings. I then had to show how to make a complete preparation and disposal of the locomotive and then it was question time! My two examiners were a Locomotive Instructor and an Engineer who just happened to have written the operating instructions for class MZ! After a few general questions, the big one came along, which involved describing the operation and working of the 'light' brake system, which is a brake used to hold the locomotive, mainly whilst shunting, and on a button being pressed, half a kilo of air is put into the brake cylinders. This was not my favourite subject and after a few minutes I had to admit that I was stuck, whereupon I was told not to worry as he, the Engineer, had taken the diagram with him, upon which he fished it out of his bag and spread it out on the driving desk. On being folded out, it was nearly as wide as the cab and after a few seconds he pointed to the diagram and said, 'You have got this far,' whereupon looking at where his finger was, I could pick up where I left off and could finally answer the question!

We were now finished with question time and went over to the station to pick up a train heading south, which I was to drive. We took over an MZ with six carriages which we were to take to Næstved, where I duly told them that I only knew the road as far as Roskilde, where the line to Kalundborg branches off, but was informed that they knew the road, so no problems. Class MZ is a direct current diesel-electric locomotive which starts with the motors in series and then when a speed of around 60km/hr is reached, power is automatically shut off, the motors switch over to parallel and power is regained, all without moving the power controller and giving a small jerk, which can be felt in the train. My Driver Instructor had always told me never to give the locomotive more than notch 6 on the power controller until it had gone into parallel working because it could be detrimental to the electrics, so this is what I did in my exam. However, after a couple of station stops, the Engineer tapped me on the shoulder and asked me what my idea was waiting to give full power until the locomotive was in parallel, and I answered with what my Instructor had told me. I got the answer that that was rubbish and that if the locomotive could not handle the changeover under full power then it would have been built differently, and I was then asked how I thought freight trains in the USA were worked with similar machines – I had no answer to that. Class MZ series 4 was also fitted with an electric dynamic brake, and one could either use the combined air/electric brake by reducing air in the brake pipe or by just the electric brake, which could be used down to about 30km/hr, finishing with the air brake. One had to have some patience with this type of locomotive as when making an initial brake application using the dynamic brake, nothing much seemed to happen at first, and one had to resist the temptation to make a heavier application because when it did react then one would be nearly sitting up in the windscreen. One eventually got used to it and it was actually a very good brake, which also matched the loco-motives' pulling power of 3900hp brute strength, which could pull a house down.

We continued to Næstved and after changing ends returned to København, with no questions whatsoever about the driving trailer and its workings. On arrival, we went up to the Instructors' office, where I was informed that I had passed and was duly presented with the appropriate certificate, the first of several I was to receive during my career. Already, the next day, I had to present myself again in København to be examined on class ME and the modified driving trailer. There was only one Instructor on my arrival, and he informed me that the other Instructor was on his way from Århus and would meet up with us at Roskilde, so it was down to the platform to take over the next westbound departure. The Instructor did not seem too interested in what I was doing as he seemed to have a lot to talk about with the booked driver, who had remained in the cab! On arrival at Roskilde, we stepped down and proceeded towards a siding where a class ME was parked and met up with our colleague from Århus. At that time, there was still a small drivers' depot of about twelve men at Roskilde where they covered the twenty-four hours with an outstationed loco-motive as a breakdown reserve as the main ground for retaining the depot. They had odd jobs in each direction from Roskilde to retain route knowledge so that they could assist wherever there occurred the need for assistance. So now I had to show how to prepare and dispose an ME and after a couple of questions returned to the station to pick up a return working to København, where I received certificate number two.

So now I was ready to take over on my own. Kalundborg depot at that time had twenty-five drivers, eighteen in the running link and seven in reserve, and the work comprised just working to København H, a distance of 117km, plus just beyond to Østerport and the carriage depot at Helgoland. With the time allowed for preparation, shunting and brake testing, plus the fact that most trains were stopping services, we could only do one return trip for a day's work even though we could have up to nine hours in a shift. As the junior at the depot, I went of course into the reserve link with no booked work and apart from rest days only knew booking on times five days in advance, which was a bit of a challenge on the home front, but I managed to make a loose agreement with the list clerk whereby she received my request each month as to how I would like to have my shifts arranged, and for the most part it worked. At this time, there were three drivers from København that lodged at our depot each weeknight working late-night trains in and earlies out, so our earliest booking on time was 04.14 and the latest booking off, apart from weekends, was 00.30. Later, we took over all finishing/starting services, which resulted in having to book off/on around 03.00 and of course an increase in the number of drivers. If one booked off after 01.30 or booked on before 04.30 then the duty was classed as a night shift, and we were only allowed to have two night shifts at a time and a maximum of seven within a four-week period. The workings were also arranged so that one rarely worked the same turn two days together, and one changed frequently from early to late shifts. Sunday was (is) part of the working week and one elected for which weekend group one wished to work in. Everything concerning rostering was arranged on the basis of seniority and at every change of the timetable there would be held a link election when one would state one's wish as regards to which link one would prefer. At our depot, there were very few of the older drivers who wished to be in the reserve link, so some time would pass before I had enough seniority to come in the running link, this being first when the depot became larger, with more link options.

MZ IV 1460, Kalundborg depot, 4/5/01

We had a small amount of freight work that comprised a night shift when we worked the last passenger service to København, returning from the main marshalling yard with an arrival in Kalundborg at 04.56 after having dropped off wagons at Holbæk as required. We also had an early turn booking on at 05.20, when we took over the incoming freight and proceeded to disperse the wagons as necessary to the various customers. These included the Statoil refinery, where we exchanged bogie tank wagons with propane gas, Danish car imports with new cars from Germany and VTG tank wagons to a smaller refinery that recycled used oil for export and other occasional freight. These jobs were booked for a class MZ but could occasionally be an ME, until one derailed on one of the harbour lines and then they were banned. After servicing all the freight customers, we made up the train for return to København which we worked as far as Holbæk, working a trip to and from the harbour there, and were then relieved by a driver from København returning to Kalundborg as passenger.

I could cover all but two duties at the depot, these involving the use of class MF (IC3) dmu's, so for the present everything I worked was loco-hauled, which suited me fine. The first couple of days were not without incident, when on my first day on the return towards Kalundborg I hit a deer (the first of many), which always had to be reported over the radio in case the animal was not dead, track staff being sent out to investigate. A couple of days later, there was some delay at Roskilde as my guard had requested police assistance with an unruly passenger. In September, there was a bomb threat at Holbæk station (flashbacks to the IRA in London in the '70s) where I had got as far as Vipperød, the last stop before Holbæk. I was called up over the radio and after receiving the information I replied that as I lived in Vipperød then I could just leave the train there, whereupon the signalman went a bit quiet and then asked me to return the train to Roskilde, which I of course did, booking back to Kalundborg as passenger with an hour's overtime but getting off the train at my home (win-win)!

A month later, I took over an eight-carriage train at København to take to Helgoland depot and then return to Kalundborg. Whilst changing ends, I glanced at the fuel gauge which on class MZ was a sight glass and could nearly not see any fuel so requested the assistance of a shunter so that I could refuel but received the answer that Helgoland was now just a multiple unit depot and that it would not be possible and that I would have to continue. I replied that if I did not receive any diesel fuel then the locomotive most likely would not get any further than Nørreport, which is a station in a tunnel. Two minutes later, there stood a shunter and I got 2000 litres of diesel to get me home, where I could fill it up ready for the next morning. This was the first of what would be many discussions during my time as a driver, nearly always managing to get the last word! The reason for the lack of fuel was twofold. First it was an MZ deputising for an ME, MZs being more thirsty and having a slightly smaller fuel capacity, and secondly the diagram had been revised during the day without taking notice of the locomotive not coming in for fuelling, an occurrence that still happens to this day.

One afternoon, I was booked to prepare an ME at Østerport for the afternoon rush hour and, having a lot of time, looked forward to having an hour or two of relaxation. However, my seat on the locomotive was defective, and as there was nobody available to repair it then I was instructed to drive light engine to the diesel depot and turn on the turntable and return to Østerport, there being just time enough to avoid a late start – so much for a quiet afternoon!

Now it was school time again as I had now received notice to attend a course for class MF. This was mainly theory, with just two days out to practise coupling/uncoupling. After passing the written exam, it was then six days with a Driving Instructor, and as we had so little work with MF in Kalundborg then I was outstationed to København. This gave me experience of driving inter-city trains to Århus, plus a day shunting with units at the maintenance depot. The following week was the practical exam, which I passed, although I did not think that it went very well. It took me a long time to feel comfortable with these units with all their computer technicalities, especially as we did not work them very often, an early turn five days a week and a late turn four days, not enough to get into a routine with them, plus the fact that we often received units that had defects keeping them from the longer runs. This proved so when on my first trip I had a thirteen-minute late start from Kalundborg because of door problems, having to isolate the defective door. So that was certificate number three.

During this period, the depot was moved to some out-of-use rooms in the station building to give us more room and to be able to accommodate female colleagues. This was okay if the duty just involved relieving at the station, but otherwise we either started in the yard in the mornings or finished there in the evenings, so it was a case of deciding on the most strategic place to park one's car.

On the night of 3rd/4th December, Denmark experienced a hurricane over most of the country, with a lot of damage and the police warning people to stay at home. On the Saturday morning I was to book on at 06.18 and so I got up earlier than normal and tuned in to the radio, where the police were still stating that one should stay home, so therefore I contacted our supervisor in København. He stated that it was not DSB's problem that I could not come to work, to which I replied that that was okay and that I would go back to bed. That got a reaction! He stated that there were three trains stranded in Jyderup station because of fallen trees and that when I deemed it safe to leave home then I could make my way to Holbæk station and sit standby, so it was obvious that it would have been completely useless to try to get to Kalundborg.

Around 07.00, I left home to see if there were any trains running. The station looked as though it had been hit by a bomb, with broken glass, overturned signage, etc. I sat for several hours at Holbæk and was then sent to København to work my booked train home. Between Roskilde and Kalundborg there were various signals and level crossings out of order with resultant delays, and it took a couple of days before everything was restored to order. Christmas was now nearly upon us and as I was in the reserve link I could choose to work either Christmas or New Year. Having children, the choice was an easy one, and so New Year's Eve I booked on at 18.31, working back with the next-to-last train arriving at Kalundborg with an arrival of 01.20. Normally, there are a lot of fireworks around midnight, but this time it was the millennium and there were fireworks practically all the way home, which was quite a sight.

Now it was back to everyday working with various hiccups along the way, of which I can give some examples. On 29th February, I prepared MZ1460 in the diesel depot in København and called up the shunter to tell him that I was ready for the traverser. When that was in position, I was called forward, and when the locomotive was halfway on, there came an ATC defect, which gave an emergency brake. It could not be released without isolating the ATC, thus rendering the locomotive a failure, so it was back to the start and prepare a replacement. One week later, I ran into some heavy rain and on starting the windscreen wiper, it parted company with its mounting and flew off into a garden, with the result of reduced speed until I came to Holbæk, where I could run the locomotive around the train, which was a one-man job as little help could be found from the guard. Just over two weeks later, there were problems again. This time, whilst driving from a driving trailer, a fault occurred with the ITC control, resulting in an emergency braking. After trying a couple of tricks, to no avail, there was nothing else to do but go to the rear end and change the cable between the carriages and the locomotive.

This was a bit of a risky business, getting down from the train and then climbing up to get a new cable from the engine room as the train had stopped on a fairly high embankment. Eventually returning to the front cab, I was relieved to see that the fault had been rectified and I could continue after getting permission from the signalman. It was fortunately a semi-fast train, which was basically a stock movement on Friday evenings so there were not many passengers, and now I could try to make up some time but, alas, just after Holbæk the same defect returned. I requested permission to change ends and return to Holbæk, but there was already a train in the next block in rear, so now I had to resort to the absolutely last solution. I informed the guard that she was now to act as driver on the locomotive whilst I would be in the front end with control over the brake. She looked rather anxious but after setting up the radio and instructing her what to do, I then returned to the front and we proceeded to Vipperød, where after the passengers were detrained we continued out onto the single line where I could change ends again and return to Holbæk, there being double track on that short section. The plan was to run the locomotive round the train and then work empty stock to København, but the brake was isolated on the resultant rear carriage. The signalman meant that I could just shunt that off and place it in a siding, but I politely (!) informed him that that would not be happening and that the train was staying where it was. I eventually got a taxi to Roskilde, where I picked up my return working. After those three incidents, I wondered what I had let myself in for and hoped that things would settle down a bit.

The class MZ locomotives were built over a period of ten years, with a total of sixty-four divided into four series. At the time that I started driving, series 3 had been withdrawn, series 4 worked in the eastern area and series 1 and 2 in the western area, but although I had only ever seen series 4, my certificate was for all MZ. In spring of 2000, the locomotive workshop in Århus was closed and all maintenance would take place in København. In May, I was booked our night turn, when we normally had the same locomotive out and back. The trip in with the last passenger was with MZ1461, and on being relieved at København H, I proceeded to the diesel depot to have my break. Whilst eating, I looked at my worksheet and discovered that my return would be with MZ1426, a series 2. That was a bit of a shock and I hoped that it had been started up and so went out with plenty of time, which was just as well as it had not been prepared. After removing the external el-cable, I climbed up and thought, *Where the hell is the battery switch?* After a bit of a look around, I found it and then I could get some light on the scene, which was totally different from a series 4. However, I did manage to prepare without having to call for help and came out onto my train on time and had a good run home, with a load of about 700tons.

On 24th July, I had my first real locomotive failure when on approaching Hvalsø station with MZ1451, there was an almighty bang from the engine room and then complete silence. On coming to a standstill, I could see a haze of smoke coming from the engine room so, taking a deep breath, I evacuated the cab (on class MZ, access to the cab was via the engine room), leaving all doors and windows open. I could diagnose that the main generator was defective and that assistance was required, which duly arrived as ME1536 from Roskilde. It was coupled onto the front of my train and after a brake test I could continue, somewhat delayed, so much so that the train was terminated at Jyderup so that it could return nearly on time. This was a period when there were many problems with the driving trailer carriages, resulting in delays, whilst placing the locomotive in front and again in København replacing the defective carriage. This was largely due to communication problems to/from the locomotive as a result of either defective cables or a defective control box.

The locomotives were also in a period of many defects as a result of intensive diagramming and not enough maintenance. The following example was typical of that period on a duty that started with a trip to Helgoland and return to København H, where on the way I had to go back to the locomotive to reset both the electric brake and energy supply on ME1523 as it wouldn't respond from the leading cab, and then on arrival at Helgoland, I received an alarm that indicated a low level of coolant, filling up 3" in the sight glass. The second half of the duty involved preparing ME1512 at the diesel depot, which had been signed off as ready for traffic. This was not the case as the locomotive had the following defects: defective radio, defective air conditioning and two defective headlights, and there was no seal on the ATC isolating switch! On making these facts known, a fitter turned up, rather grudgingly as it was Friday afternoon and near knocking-off time, and announced that he could rectify all but the air conditioning, which I would have to live with, something I was not prepared to do, but in the end he made good all the defects with just a late start of five minutes off the depot.

Towards the end of 2000, we learnt the short route out to København airport as our peak hour working with MF dmu's would be worked out to the maintenance depot before going into inter-city service. As the years went by, we would gain quite a few jobs there, usually relieving an incoming IC from Jutland and returning to be relieved again at København H. Although only just over 11 km long, it would take some time to first work out to the airport, wait for the train to be emptied and then work up to the depot, where usually after a break the procedure would be reversed. Sometimes if the depot was late in preparing the train then we would use the airport avoiding line and run ECS to regain some minutes. Not good for our customers as there were many arriving at the airport who continued their journey by train across the country.

As I mentioned earlier, Class ME was banned from working on the harbour lines at Kalundborg, but twice I booked on to relieve on the morning freight and it had arrived with an ME, but the shunters were in luck as I was certified to drive the shunting tractor, which we thus used to shunt the harbour. The amount of freight traffic was falling, sometimes only having a couple of wagons from København, but on 21st May 2001 there was an unusual amount of traffic, twenty-five wagons amounting to 997t with MZ1412. This was near the end of working freight services as DSB was to be just a passenger-carrying organisation, goods traffic being taken over by DB Railion (later DB Schenker and now DB Cargo Scandinavia). The last time that I worked a freight was on 13th June and the last time with an MZ in regular traffic two days later as all but 1401/6/25 were transferred to DB. 1401 was destined for the Danish railway museum and the two others for general breakdown rescue work.

In August, I was again involved in a great deal of discussion which began already while preparing my locomotive, ME1519, which was low on coolant. Having being filled up, it still showed on the cab panel that it was low on coolant, so I contacted the on-duty Instructor to inform him of the problem, plus the fact that according to the repair book the locomotive had a history of breakdowns with just this problem, with the consequent shutting-down of the engine. I suggested that the stock be run around so that if the problem recurred I would be sitting in the right place to start up again. He rang back to say that control had decreed that the train would run as booked, so that is what we did. About 800 metres past the section signal, the engine stopped! I contacted the signalman to say that I would proceed back to the locomotive to try and start the engine, and having done that, I requested permission to return to Kalundborg, where after a couple of minutes he informed me that it had been decided that I should continue to Værslev, where I was booked to cross a train from København and that we could transfer passengers between the two. I replied that that was not going to happen as he knew as well as I did that Værslev was just a technical station used to cross trains but without any platforms, and no way was I taking responsibility for that. He was adamant, whereupon I replied that if I did not get permission to return to Kalundborg then the train would stay where it was until he got a better idea. It took only a short while and permission was granted, and on arrival the train was declared a failure, followed up by a phone call from the Locomotive Instructor to say that he had received a reprimand over the situation, to which I replied that he should just give me the phone number so that I could put my case forward, but he did not think that would be a good idea as he could hear what frame of mind I was in.

Looking through my diaries, I can see that not one month went by without some sort of defect and delay, 2002 being especially bad, it being said that somebody at the central workshops had decided on a new type of lubricating oil for class ME against the recommendation of General Motors, with the result that there occurred many failures. One such day was 1st August, when on waiting at Holbæk for a train to go to work, I was contacted to say that I should stay where I was as my train had failed on its way to Kalundborg and that there was a locomotive on its way that I should relieve on and work to Mørkøv where my train was waiting, couple on and drag it all to København as my booked train. MZ1406 turned up and that was the absolutely last time that I drove a member of this class, so now all our work was mainly ME with some MF, but soon we were to witness a little revolution when DSB decided to lease double-deck stock built by Bombardier, which also resulted in modifying some ME to be able to run with ZWS control and to be able to control the train's doors from the cab. As the new stock was painted grey and dark blue then the locomotives were also repainted blue.

Another interesting discussion took place with control one day after arrival at Helgoland. I had just changed ends and luckily was standing entering information in the ATC box when the air conditioning system emptied itself with ice-cold water onto my seat. I rang in to explain the situation, whereupon after a few minutes I received the reply that a shunter would be coming over to me with a plastic sack to drape over the seat. My answer to that was that if the controller thought that I was going to sit on a plastic sack all the way to Kalundborg on a hot summer day then he could think again, as I could just as well sit on the soaking-wet seat. I would take it to København H and no further. He tried to argue, but when I asked him if he would sit on a defective office chair then he had to agree with my argument.

In July, we gained some work along the coastline from København to Helsingør as a result of engineering work at Østerport, which involved closing the carriage sidings there and therefore having to run the ECS to/from Helsingør. We actually retained work on this route for six years, generally working peak hour semi-fast trains to Helsingør and returning as ECS. Today, learning a new route can be quite an affair with having to ride with a driving instructor and passing a test on an iPad. On my first day, I had a pilotman to/from Helsingør and after that you were on your own if you felt okay with it. The route was equipped with ATC, which of course was a great help, and one always had the working timetable open on the desk. This gave added variety to our duties, which was very welcome.

During the spring of 2002, our union announced a study trip to Italy to view the construction of the new inter-city dmu stock that had been ordered from Ansaldo Breda, which members would be invited to apply for. It would be in September and there would be three trips organised and all depots were to be represented, and if there were too many applications then lots would be drawn. We were only two from Kalundborg who had applied, so we secured our place on one of the trips. We would be travelling by train, which proved to be a bit of a marathon with an early start to a twenty-four hour journey, arriving at Torino, where we could see the new diesel engines at the Iveco factory and where we also heard a lecture from a company director whose English was not too good, resulting in a fight to stay awake!

The next day, we travelled to Firenze and then out to Ansaldo Breda in Pistoia to see the construction of both underframes and body shells, plus a mock-up of the driver's cab. It was a very informative trip but with no inkling of the coming problems that would follow the introduction of the new trains to traffic. The company was not exactly an expert in building diesel trains, and the general opinion is that they should never have been built, but when politics get mixed up in state-run businesses then it is always a recipe for near disaster. There were ordered eighty-two four-car and twenty-three two-car units because at that time the government would not offer money for electrification, one of the bigger scandals in this country, one might say. On one of my first visits to Denmark I had seen a brochure from DSB announcing that electrification of all main lines would be complete by 1999, but here in 2024 we are still some way off that goal, which goes to show that whatever type of government is in office, be it to the left or right, then they do not really give a shit about public transport.

The new double-deck stock was beginning to arrive and so it was back to school, which sounds rather grand but it was a rather nondescript affair. The instruction involved first a theory day at Roskilde, which was a bit of a farce as it turned out. The plan was to operate the new stock with class ME locomotives, but as none could be given free from traffic then an electric locomotive of class EA was coupled to a driving trailer, which was a waste of time as the ZWS control system built in the new stock was not compatible with the older version on the locomotive, this state of affairs lasting for many years until the remaining class EA were modified. This meant that when opening up the cab of the driving trailer, many faults would show up, so coupled with the fact that the Instructor did not really know a lot about the new stock, the day was not particularly useful.

At first, it would just be Kalundborg depot, plus a number of drivers from København who would be trained. Just over a month later, I was booked for one day's practical training with a Driving Instructor, which was also a bit special as the train we were to use was formed of an ME locomotive with a driving trailer coupled to each end so that we could experience driving from the ABS as they are known in both directions on the route chosen, which was Roskilde – Ringsted – Næstved. As only two ZWS systems can be active at any one time, the trailing ABS had to be set neutral each time, and as that was an abnormal procedure then it was a good idea if the trainee was not shown what was going on. My Instructor sent me out of the cab each time, but that was not always the case with the others, and consequently in the beginning, quite a few mistakes were made when changing ends. The new system was a lot different from the existing ITC system as, for example, if there was a need for two locomotives then they had to be placed at each end of the train if they were both to be active and the ABS completely shut down. The old system allowed two locomotives at one end of the train to both be controlled from the driving trailer. This at first also caused a bit of confusion with control of the doors as when arriving at a station, it was now the driver that had to give the doors free on stopping, which was not a problem with the normal train formation but if for some reason the locomotive was in front of the ABS then each carriage had to be reset, or else when the driver released the doors to the right he would actually be releasing to the opposite side, which was not a particularly good thing! It was good to get some brand-new stock which was generally problem-free, if you subtract driver error, the older stock still giving technical problems.

In the first fourteen days of November alone it was necessary for me on three occasions to run the locomotive around because of driver trailer defects. My debut with the new stock alone was on 2nd December, and then some more instruction was to come our way. DSB had got a good idea, in their view, to save money by decreeing that the new stock would be in fixed formations of either an ME plus four or six carriages, and all servicing would be carried out in Køben-havn as a complete set, thus saving on shunting staff. This would mean that the drivers would take over the daily carriage inspection at night and would also be responsible for filling the water tanks and toilet tank emptying, plus on parking the trains coupling the 1500v external electric supply, for which we received one day's instruction. Where the savings were, nobody has understood as we received extra duties to cover this work, plus the fact that a small number of shunters were retained as we still had some of the older stock parked at Kalundborg at night. Extra time was also allotted to our duties for washing the trains as this would now be done by the main line loco-motive. The redundant shunters were offered the chance to be trained as drivers, a handful passing the necessary exams. The result of all this was that we had a shortage of drivers and for a couple of years had a fairly large contingent on loan from Aarhus depot. Later, it was found that the six-carriage formations could also be used at the weekends instead of lying spare, so two carriages could be taken out on Friday evening and replaced again Sunday evening, which resulted in DSB having to recruit new shunting staff, and after a while they resumed the tasks we had previously taken from them, so instead of a saving, I think most probably that it has cost DSB more. All this would be reversed again later (!), especially after receiving more dmu stock, of which more later in this narrative. The double-deck stock gave very few problems, mostly because in my opinion the stock was not owned but leased, thus barring DSB from trying to make any 'modifications' to them. Many years later, they would be purchased from the lessors.

It was about this time that my group leader approached me to ask if I would be interested in becoming a Driver Instructor as at that time we only had two at the depot, and he thought that I would be suitable for the job. I would have to sit a selection exam, which I did on 27th February 2003. It was quite a hard day, with various written tests, an instruction test, where I had to instruct a given subject, and then an interview, which I passed, and already a month later I was sent on my first course, the first of several in the coming years. There is one thing about working on the railways: one never stops learning.

According to my notebooks, 2003 seems to have been a quiet year, except for 23rd September. On this day, I booked on at 05.44, with no inkling that it would be 22.30 before booking off again! I had worked the first half of my duty and had begun the second part when having just left Helgoland carriage sidings on time, all signals went out and there I was stuck between stations, luckily with empty stock. It transpired that there had been a complete power cut over the whole of eastern Denmark, and there I stood for the next five hours. When things started to move again, it took ages to reach København H as there were trains at every signal, and every arrival had to be sorted out as to where it was going and with which staff, and on arrival, I was asked what I intended to do, but as I could ascertain that there were no relief drivers or taxis available, I offered to drive the train to Kalundborg, that being the quickest way to get home. The Foreman had the cheek to ask me if I would be coming in the next day for my booked turn, to which I replied, 'Not on your life,' or words to that effect, so it was ten hours' overtime and an extra rest day as a result.

My first day as Driving Instructor with the first of many trainees that I would have during the next sixteen years was 17th November. My first trainee was nearly my last as he was not an easy one by a long way. He came from the S-trains so it was a traction course, and it was so difficult to get a word out of him that I was on the point of giving up, but talking with an older Instructor in København, he informed me that my trainee was one of the worst he had experienced over many years so I stuck it out. In all the time that he remained with DSB, he was a very difficult person to communicate with.

Our group leader up to this time had been based in København, having both a group of drivers there plus Kalundborg depot. This was to change now as DSB had decided that each depot would have its own local leader, and ours was to be one of our own local

Instructors. This I felt was not a particularly smart move as he was a bit too 'friendly' with many of the other drivers and also gave the impression that he had only taken the job to have a fixed day job and a better pension. It also proved later that he was not very well suited to the job, and if one experienced a problem out on the track then nothing really happened until it was too late to have any consequence. He had also been cashier in our local union branch, a position which thus became open at the AGM on 28th January 2004, to which I was elected without opposition (!) and which I would hold for the next ten years. Our committee consisted of three members, chairman, vice-chairman and cashier. Over and above the AGM we would occasionally hold a members' meeting if anything radical was to be discussed, and we would have 'office' days for the committee, DSB providing an office with computer, printer, etc.,etc., at the depot. Being active within the union gave a lot of inside information, especially regarding the future of the depot and its work content. We also had quite a sum of money in the bank, receiving a contribution from the union head office each year, which was to cover the cost of the AGM amongst other things. The AGM was always held at the station restaurant, with a meal afterwards, where our local pensioned members were also invited. Later on, as I will come to relate, we also tried to use some of the money to finance social arrangements for our members so that we did not have too much standing in the account.

I have not recorded very much for 2004 so it must have been a quiet year, when the only thing of note was that in November we had some days giving our colleagues supplementary information concerning the double-deck stock.

In 2005/06, we were kept busy with trainee drivers, also trainees from København as there was a shortage of Driving Instructors there, and that was not without various incidents. The first was a breakdown where the locomotive had decided to rid itself of lubricating oil, thus shutting the engine down. The trainee at that time was also a bit of a problem, with several issues on the home front resulting in a lack of concentration, which affected his judgement when approaching stop signals and in the end, after my recommendation to my group leader, his employment was terminated. This resulted in me getting a visit from one of the training school Instructors to tell me that the trainee had lodged a complaint against me, trying to say that I had sent him home early on several occasions and therefore he had not received the required training! DSB did not accept his complaint as we as Driving Instructors were trusted to carry out our duties to the letter. I have always adhered to the principle that when passing on a trainee I would have no problem with letting my grandchildren ride in a train that he/she was driving, and if I was in doubt then I would refer them to my group leader.

The next incident was with another trainee and was on a journey from Kalundborg, where about halfway between stations we received a fire alarm. My trainee immediately went to brake the train, to which I said that she should refrain as we should stop at a point where it would be easy for the fire brigade to attend. I looked back out of the window and could not see either smoke or flames coming from the locomotive so decided that we should continue to the next station. On arriving at Svebølle, the diesel engine had also shut down and as we had a few minutes to spare waiting to cross a train from København, we informed the signalman of what had occurred and said we would investigate the problem. On getting back to the loco-motive, we could see that there was no fire but that an electrical cabinet in cab number 2 had had a meltdown, so the locomotive was a failure. We therefore made it ready for transport 'dead in train' and then awaited instructions. The train we should cross had departed to Kalundborg and would return an hour after our arrival and would take our passengers. It was then decided that the next arrival from København would come as empty stock from the preceeding station to couple onto us, and then we could work the whole train to København. This was really good stuff for my trainee and she learnt a lot that day, especially as our train consisted of five of the old carriages and the rescue train had four double-deckers, which was interesting to brake as it was a mix of traditional air brake plus EP-brake on the DD stock.

As stated, I had several trainees from København, one of which was destined to become an Instructor. He came to Kalundborg to be trained on class ME as we had so much work on them and were regarded by some as experts! On the first day, we left Kalundborg with six of the older Bn stock, with the ME at the rear of the train as normal. The older driving trailers had a bench seat on the second-man's side, where I sat, and we were rapidly approaching Svebølle station where we were booked to cross. Between Kalundborg and Holbæk there is no ATC, which means that when a signal shows entrance to the station with a speed restriction then that starts from the signal, whereas with ATC the system will give a braking curve to the danger point. We were travelling at about 110km/t and Søren was showing no intention of braking until I asked where the shown 60km/t started, to which he reacted rather quickly, bringing the train into the station safely at the correct speed. He had been driving for two years but only on routes with ATC, so it was really a wake-up call. He was amazed at how relaxed I had been, but I assured him that I would have intervened if he hadn't reacted to my question. Everytime we met thereafter, he always mentioned that day – he never forgot.

I have only had two trainees that I have not been able to recommend to go further with their training. The first I have mentioned and the second was a bit of a special case. He had come from another depot where there had been some problems, and now he was at Kalundborg, where he had to learn class ME. His problem was that I could ask him to study a particular subject which the next day he could repeat word for word, but he could just not put it into practice. He had big problems with starting the diesel motor each time, pressing the hand throttle right in, resulting in far too many revolutions so that the overspeed tripped. The noise was incredible! I requested some extra days before sending him up for his exam but he failed, as I had expected, and after a few days with another Driving Instructor he failed again, and thus his employment was terminated, whereupon he also tried to complain that he had not been treated fairly!

We had decided on the union committee to try and organise a study trip with a subsidy from our funds. This was to be the first of several, and we decided that Berlin would be a good place to start. We would travel by train, with two nights in a hotel. This first trip was not so ambitious, with just a visit to the technical museum as the main attraction, but it was a great success, with ten members taking part, the size of the depot decreeing how many could be away at one time.

An interesting day, though not for our passengers, occurred in June 2006 when there had been a thunderstorm when lightning had put all signals between Kalundborg and Holbæk out of action, with all of them showing 'Stop'. This meant that one had to be advised by the signalman over the radio to pass each signal at danger, resulting in dropping thirty minutes in the schedule, and several crossing barriers also had to be activated manually, but all was well again on returning during the afternoon.

Our next study trip was in October 2006, and this time we went to Dresden, staying three nights there. I had managed to make contact with Bombardier's carriage factory in Gørlitz where our DD stock was built, and we received a very fine tour, seeing a lot of new stock in various stages of construction. Dresden is a fine city with a lot to see, and we managed to include a paddle steamer trip on the river Elb. Our last evening, we had found a good restaurant where the branch funds would finance the food and our group leader would pay for the drinks. What little respect I had left for him went out the window on this occasion as he protested when not everybody wanted beer but some would like to share a bottle of wine! What the hell difference that made I do not know, but after the dust had settled, they got their wine as, after all, it was pointed out that it was not being paid for out of his own pocket, and actually I suspected him of collecting other peoples' receipts to feather his own nest. Now the meal was under way and it was mentioned that there was an Irish pub close by that we could visit afterwards for some Guinness. I happened also to hear one whisper that he would try to drink 'the Englishman' under the table, but luckily I had chosen a relatively solid meal and was prepared, thus after ten pints we had to carry my opponent back to the hotel!

The year 2007 didn't offer a lot of excitement, with just a day with a lot of delays as the result of a fatality, resulting in overtime and a taxi home as the last train had departed, two failures with class ME, one being a lack of motor oil and one with a seized wheelset, and a fire alarm on a class MF dmu, which was of course on the rearmost carriage of a five-set formation (300 metres) and in the morning rush hour, but the offending set had shut down the engine and neutralised the gear, so just a bit of morning exercise! However, one incident comes to mind which shows how incompetent our group leader was. It was Sunday, 1st July and I arrived at Valby, the last stop before København H. On receiving the signal to start from the guard, the warning lights for the doors were still blinking, which meant that I may not proceed as per operating instructions. I got the guard to check all doors but the result was the same, so I contacted the signalling centre and then the duty Instructor, and now it gets interesting. After a brief discussion, he referred to a new instruction that should give responsibility of the doors to the guard, and if the doors had been checked then I could proceed. I had just returned from three weeks' holiday and became unsure that I had overseen a new instruction so proceeded to København. As soon as the train began to move, the warning lamps stopped blinking! There was a delay of thirteen minutes, with a queue of trains building up behind. On arrival at København, I went up to the Instructor to try and clear the matter up. I demanded to see the new instruction and after some dithering he referred me to a paragraph that had absolutely nothing to do with DD-stock but with the external door lamps on the older stock. I felt that I had been duped into moving my train against current regulations and had a very low opinion of said Instructor.

On arrival back at Kalundborg, I submitted my report to our group leader; a complete waste of time as the resulting correspondence showed. The duty Instructor's version was of course totally different to mine as he was trying to cover his back, and most of the discussion was concentrated on how much time had been lost, with the allegation that I had taken far too long before making contact with the 'outside world'. My group leader did not apparently take my report seriously, and he let the case drag on so long that in the end I gave up, knowing inwardly that I was right. At the end of the year, the depot was moved out to a building by the carriage sidings, which was much more central with respect to our duties. By this time, our group leader had retired, and we then had a rather turbulent time as it was apparently not so easy to recruit a replacement to our neck of the woods and didn't stabilise until about 2009.

An interesting incident occurred one Sunday afternoon in August 2008 when, having just booked on, the driver that I should relieve came into the room to tell me that the train was up at the station and that there was a problem with the driving trailer. The steps up into the cab had collapsed, and he asked me to contact our supervisor in København as to what I intended to do. I phoned in and said that I was not prepared to take the train as it was but came with a possible solution, which was to prepare a locomotive standing in the carriage sidings and couple it to the front of my train and work it with a locomotive at each end with a delay of about twenty minutes. After he had referred to control, my plan was agreed and we got away with a seventeen-minute delay and with a guard who was quick off the mark at each station and 6600hp available together with the electric brake on both locomotives. The train was running on time by the time we were halfway through the journey.

In 2008, our study trip was to Germany again, this time to the island of Rügen and again for three nights and staying in the town of Bergen in the middle of the island. In the programme this time was a trip on the narrow gauge steam railway from Putbus to Göhren, returning as far as Binz, where we had lunch in the station restaurant, which was decorated as though one was sitting in a carriage. We also visited Prora, where there exists an enormous building complex that was constructed by Hitler's regime as a holiday paradise for the working class and which extends for 4-5 km and just 150 metres from sandy beaches. It is so solidly built that demolishing it has shown not to be an option. At that time, it housed a small museum describing the original project, plus a technical museum in a former workshop building which housed both rail and road vehicles. Otherwise, all the buildings were empty. After World War II, it had housed a contingent of the Russian Red Army and later the East German NVA. Now some of the buildings have been converted to luxury holiday apartments and a youth hostel.

We have now reached 2009, which started in January with an

operation for a hernia, which gave me a fortnight off work until I could climb up to a locomotive from the ground again. The group leader who was holding the chair at that time had asked me if I was interested in applying for the job, to which I declined, giving the reason that as a Driving Instructor I had achieved all that I wanted and enjoyed driving trains, plus the fact that I had no wish to reduce my earnings as at that time the group leaders had not negotiated their status as yet and therefore earned less than me! I had also been asked if I was interested in being an Instructor at the training school but declined that also, it being much more fun driving trains.

Some information regarding braking and brake force is now relevant. All locomotives and stock were provided with a three-way switch, a so called G-P-R, where G stands for goods slow working brake, P for passenger faster working brake and R, which stands for passenger fast and more effective brake. This brake means that at higher speeds when braking, there is double pressure in the brake cylinders, reducing to the half when under 60 km/hr to smooth out the braking. All passenger trains are normally in 'R' but must not exceed 400 metres in length and give a high brake force, for example, an ME with four DD has a brake force of 130% and all goods trains are in 'P'. All locomotive-hauled trains have to have a valid hand-written brake slip on the driver's desk alongside the working timetable; this is the responsibility of the driver who has carried out the brake test. It is valid for twenty-four hours, but if the train is reformed during the day then a new slip has to be filled out and the former thrown away as only one may be found at any one time, and of course when changing direction then the slip follows.

We had lost our work to Helsingør in May 2008 but now in September 2009 we had to learn the route from Roskilde to Ring-sted, a distance of around 30km, in preparation for the new timetable in December, when we received a couple duties using ME + DD, not learning EMU stock until much later. Also in September there occurred a tragic accident just outside of Tølløse station, where in foggy weather a large truck failed to stop at the level crossing barriers and drove out in front of the first train from Kalundborg, which was formed of a single class MF dmu, with the result that the

Driver Instructor received a broken back and his young trainee died of internal injuries. This was a great shock for both the depot and the railway community in general, which we could see by the amount of colleagues who attended the funeral.

I have recorded in my notes that during this period there were many problems with class MF, in particular, isolated motors. They have four motors in each set, two classified as 'A' motor, which have a generator and a compressor attached, and two 'B' motors, which only deliver power, so there always has to be at least one 'A' motor active. If there is an 'A' motor inactive and one only has a single set then when preparing it can take up to twenty-five minutes to pump up the air supply, and as there was only allotted ten minutes then time was already critical.

The first half of the year 2010 was relatively quiet ... until I missed a station! I had misread the working timetable and in the morning rush hour failed to stop at Trekroner station. At the previous stop I had been joined in the cab by a colleague on his way to book on in København,and on the approach to Trekroner he asked me if we were to stop there and I replied no, adding that it would be too late now anyway! There were a lot of prospective customers on the platform but I could see that the monitors showed 'Beware of passing train', so no panic. The guard was very quick to come out and inform me of my mistake, but there was no reaction from the signalling control centre even though we arrived at the next station a bit before the booked time and in fact we heard no more of the incident for the rest of the journey. On my return journey to Kalundborg, our group leader joined me at Høje Taastrup for a routine cab visit and after the usual small talk he stated that DSB had started a campaign to find out why the number of stations being missed was on the increase! I replied that there were 'perhaps too many variations in the timetable and that I had missed a station that very morning, enlarging on my idea by saying that the actual train numbers could lead one astray, although I had no excuse for my lapse of concentration when reading the timetable. On our route, the normal stopping services were numbered 25xx, the semi-fast services 15xx and the 'odd' rush-hour/out-of-hours services 45xx, but in several instances extra stops were put in without the number being changed, when really anything out of the norm should have been a 45xx number. He said that I should be more careful in future and left it at that. In the whole of my career, I have missed four stations; two in England and two in Denmark, far less than some.

In the early hours of Monday, 5th July there occurred a fire at Holbæk station in a relay hut that completely destroyed the signalling system there, with the resulting chaos to follow. For the first month, the preceding stations on both sides of Holbæk were manned and each train was issued with a form S1 before being allowed to proceed, this telling the driver that all signals between the stations were to be ignored. After this first month, a form of control was established at Holbæk station, whereupon on stopping at the home signal we would be verbally instructed in and out of the station, this situation lasting until January 2013! One had to keep very alert because as the time passed the situation became very much routine, with the risk of making a mistake increasing. It took so long to establish a new system because supplies of relay-based signalling apparatus were a bit thin on the ground, and a redundant example from another station had to be modified and installed.

Since becoming a member of the union committee, I had acquired a couple of extra tasks; one having new items for the uniform programme on trial and the other to read corrections to the working instructions for ME + DD. I was now asked by my group leader if I would like to join a punctuality group, to which I agreed. It would comprise representatives from all involved parties with the aim of improving punctuality on Northwest Railway, to which our route was known. It was a day off from driving each time we held a meeting and we had a lot of interesting discussions, managing to make quite a few adjustments and improving timekeeping, which very often left us at the top of the monthly results.

So, time for a study trip again, and this time it would be to England, and as the time taken by train through Europe and eventually the Channel Tunnel would be much too long, we would now be flying to Gatwick and then travelling by train to Victoria. We had found a hotel near Paddington; it did not have many stars, if any, but was well placed for getting around. The first job after a couple of pints was to go to King's Cross and book seats for the next morning to York and return as we were to visit the Railway Museum, all travelling on our international free passes. On arrival at York, three of us went in search of a pub that could serve food for us early evening before catching the train back. I decided that we should just order a mixed grill for everyone, which is what we did, the pub not even wanting a deposit. We had a very agreeable day at the museum and then proceeded to the pub, where they served up one of the biggest mixed grills I had ever seen, washed down with some good Yorkshire ale. The next day was to be the highlight of the trip as I had made contact with a former colleague who was now in the employ of ASLEF to help making arrangements. We met at Selhurst station and after being signed in were shown around parts of the depot and some of the rolling stock, class 377 EMU, 172 DMU and 73 electro-diesel locomotives. After finishing there, the next destination was the ASLEF headquarters in Arkwright Road, Hampstead, where we were very well received and shown around the building, which had actually just been sold as the upkeep was getting rather expensive. I had been informed that the union would be our hosts for a light lunch, which proved to be a bit more than that so, having exchanged gifts, we were escorted to a pub just round the corner and told that we could order whatever we would like to eat from the menu, and then the ale started to flow and continued all afternoon, any attempt to buy a round swept away with the retort that it was us that were the guests. It was good that we were first returning home in the late afternoon/evening the next day!

The winter of 2010 proved to be a cold one, with a lot of snow at Christmas. On 23rd December, I booked on at 15.24 and on taking over the train I tested the horn, which on DD stock is placed behind a small grill under the buffer beam, as I could see that it was clogged with ice and snow. There came no sound from it whatsoever and it was impossible to clear it, so therefore I contacted København to inform them of the situation, and it was decided that I should shunt the train to the carriage sidings to run round the stock, not being possible at the platforms at Kalund-borg, which was not as easy as it sounds. There were two shunters to help me, but it took nearly an hour as the couplings between the locomotive and carriages were one solid bar of ice. The points had to be freed of snow and then when having manoeuvred the locomotive to the other end, the couplings were also frozen and took some persuading before they could be used. Having taken so much time, I departed in the plan of the next departure as the driver of that train had the same problem as me. My return working was cancelled because of a shortage of stock – I wonder why – so home as passenger with an early finish, my car luckily not being at Kalundborg that day.

The next day, Christmas Eve, which is the most important day at Christmas in Denmark, I was booked on to work at around 20.00, finishing with the next-to-last service from København, and for this I was to work a single class MF dmu. It had snowed again and on having passed through Værslev and out onto the single line again, I encountered a large snowdrift at 120km/hr, rocking the train considerably but getting through, and informed the signalman to warn the driver of the last train. The next day, I could see the perfect outline of my train in the snow! The roads were also bad, taking me over an hour to drive home instead of forty minutes.

On Sunday, 23rd January, I was working a late afternoon train to København when after passing Glostrup and travelling at about 150km/hr, I saw a movement from a pathway just the other side of the fence; two people walking, when one of them suddenly threw a large object, which appeared to be a lump of metal. All this happened in a split second and although registering what was happening, I did not manage to get out of my seat. There was an almighty crash and there appeared a large crack/star across the windscreen. Luckily, it held, but I could feel a large dent on the inside of the glass. I had of course braked the train but continued driving at a lower speed whilst contacting the signalman and then our supervisor. The train was taken out of service on arrival, and I was asked if I felt well enough to continue my duty, to which I replied in the affirmative but was told that if I suddenly felt unwell then there was a spare man who could cover, but it was not necessary.

Around this time there were two new technical items that were to be introduced. Firstly a system called 'Greenspeed', which consisted of a screen in the cab which after the ATC data was plotted in could calculate the optimal speed to proceed at to keep time and was supposed to make a saving on diesel oil, but as most drivers already drove economically then the savings were minimal. We had always been trained to give full gas on starting, allowing the train to drift when the required speed was reached and then just enough to maintain speed, which was also good for the diesel engine as it would get full effect from the turbo. Greenspeed was also seen as a spy in the cab, which was not exactly welcome.

The second innovation was the conversion of hand-operated points to electric, with an operating box at cab level so that the driver had no need to leave the cab each time. Coupled to the points was a new form of shunt signal showing the direction chosen, and the other boxes in the same area showed a red light, signifying that a route had already been set up. There occurred mishaps from time to time when if a train rolled past the signal then the whole area would be blocked until the system was reset. Each of these new systems required one day of instruction.

Another new innovation was an adjustment to the ground course for new entrants where they would now have to pass a practical exam already at the end of the second module to attain their licence. I do not know why this alteration was made as the licence could not be used before traction training and route learning had taken place, but it had now been decided and the exam would be carried out by the Driver Instructor, along with an Instructor from the school as censor. In August, I therefore had my first trainee to examine and, although it was not so intimidating, having only to go through the procedures of booking on, preparing the cab and then driving, it was enough to set his nerves on edge, but it all went off well.

In March 2012, there came a call from the training school to learn a 'new' class of traction, class MR dmu. This was a class dating from the late 1970s and based on the DB class 628 and comprised two motorised carriages, being capable of working in multiple with up to five sets. They have always traditionally been based in the western part of the country with only limited use in the east. The reason for us having to learn them was that it had been decided to convert our route between Vipperød and Lejre to double track, which would mean a complete closure from Holbæk for a period of around three months, three years in a row, and we would just be running a shuttle service between Kalundborg and Holbæk. We would be allocated twelve MR sets, which would be maintained by travelling fitters using the former carriage workshop although only having the need for four to six sets each day, leaving ample cover for maintenance as reliability for these elderly trains did not have a good reputation.

The only depot in our region to use these trains was Næstved, and therefore all practical training was with Driving Instructors from that depot, with us being outstationed. The static training was to take place in Kalundborg, where two sets were provided as we also had to learn to couple them in multiple, this being the driver's job, just like with locomotives. Having completed the training, I received my MR certificate on 14th May, ready for the shutdown to start at the beginning of June. Then I received a bit of a shock as I was already marked up to have a trainee with me after only having two days alone with this newly acquired knowledge, which I thought was a bit much. However, I was in luck as we had very recently got a new group leader at Kalundborg, Tommy Jørgensen, and I contacted him to say that I did not feel competent to have a trainee for MR as yet. Now Tommy had earlier in his career been a driver at Næstved depot and had a lot of experience with said trains, and all he said in reply was 'Can you meet me at Næstved next Tuesday at nine o'clock?'

The next day, I was marked up to go to Næstved the following week and I duly met Tommy there, whereupon he announced that he was my trainee for the day and that he was quite new to class MR. We proceeded over to the stabling point where I had to instruct him in both preparation and disposal of two sets coupled together, where he confronted me with a lot of questions to which as he had not been a driver for some years I had to reply, supplementing with the alterations to operating instructions which had come since then. When we were finished, he said that he had made arrangements to give a Næstved driver an early day and we would work his train to Roskilde and return, where I had to instruct him how to drive! On returning to Næstved, he just asked me if I now felt confident to have a trainee with me, to which I replied in the affirmative. During the day, I found out that this man was the driver of the train I had derailed at Helgoland, about which we had a good laugh (not funny at the time). I thought that we now had a group leader I could respect, and this proved to be the case until I retired.

The work at the depot was, for some, rather tedious now, although I enjoyed it as we saw a lot more of our own colleagues with all breaks being held at the depot, plus there was an increase in spare turns. Some of the duties involved three round trips to Holbæk but mostly just two, and some just involved preparation/disposal and shunting to/from the workshop area. The social aspect had improved as we generally had mealtimes together, and our outdoor grill was in use most evenings. The only downside was that we had a couple of colleagues who seemed to take great delight in finding faults so as to be able to take a set out of traffic, which although it was sometimes justified it went a bit over the top, coming to the notice of the workshop chief at Fredericia, where all MR sets were allocated. Many of the faults they had found were neither safety orientated nor prevented completion of the diagrammed work and were just a nuisance for the rest of us, suddenly finding ourselves having to prepare a replacement at short notice. It was the 24th August and we were back to normal again, and now it was soon time for a study trip again, the last that I would be arranging.

I had decided that we would make a return to England and got started on research to see where we should go. The result was a flight to Gatwick again with train to Victoria, transfer to St Pancras and then a quick trip up to Derby. Once again, a cheap hotel near the centre and we were all set. I had made arrangements with East Midlands Trains for a tour of Etches Park depot, for which they had stated that they could accommodate us for about ninety minutes. On arrival at the depot gates, we were all signed in and then escorted to a meeting room where we received a brief rundown from the depot manager of the aims of the depot and of the company as a whole before we were handed over to our guide. At each of our places at the table we were presented with a folder describing the rolling stock fleet, depot layout and a description of a typical twenty-four hours at the depot, together with a depot coffee mug. The tour of the depot turned out to be much more comprehensive than we had anticipated and took the best part of three hours, when we had an opportunity to see all the different train types, the various workshops and the wheel lathe in action. Altogether a good day, just managing to make the pub and chip shop before closing time!

For the evening, I had arranged a pub crawl where we were collected outside the hotel in a minibus and then proceeded to six different pubs, finishing up at the Exeter Arms, where the Paul Evans Trio (no relation) blues band were playing; a really great evening. The next day was completely different, seeing us take the local train to Whatstandwell and then walking a couple of miles to Crich Tramway Museum, the weather being very kind to us, so the walk through some fantastic scenery was on the whole no problem, apart from a couple of the group having to stop for a 'blow-up' after negotiating a particularly steep hill! The museum was well worth the visit, and so was Derby, a town with many interesting buildings and a lot of good pubs. That was my last study trip and in my opinion the best of them, which has been confirmed by those who took part as it was still a talking point on my retirement seven years later.

The year 2013 was to be a year totally different from all others. It started off quite normally with not a lot out of the ordinary and then a refresher course for class MR, ready for the summer shutdown again. On 20th April, I attended a colleague's sixtieth birthday at a Chinese restaurant in Kalundborg, not drinking as I was driving and not getting home late. After a good night's sleep and breakfast, my wife and I had some gardening to do when suddenly I was lying in some bushes, and the next couple of hours have been totally blank for me ever since. An ambulance took me to hospital, where a lot of tests were carried out; the first memory for me being when taken from the casualty room up to a ward. I was monitored for the rest of the day and then sent home, having had a type of epileptic fit. I rang my group leader to inform him of what had happened, who said that I was now grounded indefinitely. The coming week I was sent for scans, which gave no result, but it was decided that I was forbidden to drive both car and trains for the next six months. I was then in contact with my workplace again, and we agreed that I could come to the depot and do any odd jobs that could be found so that I could keep in contact with my colleagues. I could come and go as I pleased as long as my group leader knew where I was, which made it a lot easier for making doctors' appointments, etc. It was a long six months but it was during the summer and autumn period, so it could have been worse.

One of the jobs I landed in was to paint yellow stripes along all our walkways in the station and yard areas after having shown our leader an air-photo of some depot areas in the UK, which he took up at once as a good idea, sending me off to the local paint store to order the necessary paint, brushes, etc. I could do it as I saw fit, so there was no stress involved and the time went quite quickly, but no driving with class MR that year. I eventually got the green light to drive again, having not had any repetition of epilepsy and no require-ments for medicine. To be able to start again, I had to have two days out with a Driving Instructor and then undergo a rules test, and then it was back on the track alone again. During the year, the rest of the depot had received traction training on class ER EMU sets as we were to work them on our duties to Ringsted, of which we were to have more. For obvious reasons, I could not partake and so until I could be accommodated on a course whenever I had such a duty then that part would be covered by the list clerk and I would sit spare at København until I could work back to Kalundborg.

In February, I arrived back at the depot to be met by my leader and a photographer to have pictures taken and be interviewed for DSB's internal magazine in connection with my twenty-five-year jubilee. This had been arranged by my leader as he was always very keen to put our depot on the map to show who we were and what we could do, which he had also done the first year that we had class MR when he had a journalist from the local newspaper ride in the cab with him and me to Holbæk, with an article with photos being published. Now it was 2014 and a busy year for me as already in March I attended the training school for class ER followed immediately after with a brush-up day on class MR. The next month, I was outstationed in København with a Driving Instructor, finishing with the practical test, which I thought was a tough one. The ER sets can work in multiple with MF dmu's, and I never really felt at ease with either type, which was probably because we never had so much work with them to build up a routine, but as they were reasonably trouble-free it helped with time. The day after the test I had an introduction day on class MG dmu sets, which are the infamous Italian-built trains that were supposed to have been the new generation intercity stock but had generally been relegated to regional train workings, and we were to have them in Kalundborg. We were now locked in again, so along with the twelve MR sets, we also had two MG sets for training purposes. Again, it was outstationing in København for the practical driving part of the course, and on 11th June, I received my certificate and then it was back to the Holbæk shuttle service until the end of August, when the double tracking was now complete between Holbæk and Roskilde. On 1st July, I celebrated twenty-five years with DSB with an open-house arrangement at the station restaurant, where family and many colleagues attended and I received many gifts. Tommy, my group leader, gave a speech specifying my career with DSB and of course bringing up the derailment we had both been involved with. He also presented me with copies of all the correspondence I had with DSB during those twenty-five years.

According to my notebooks, the next year was very quiet, only noting two occasions when there was a shortage of driving trailers and therefore having a locomotive at each end instead, making life very easy to make up any lost time. We were gaining a lot of experience with class MG, which had a lot of faults, although mercifully with few complete failures. Then in September2015, I attended the yearly medical, with the result that I was taken off driving again with high blood pressure, which lasted a month until the medicine kicked

Class MR at Kalundborg, 16/8/14

in. In December, it was route learning again as the half-hourly Ringsted service would be extended to Slagelse on an hourly basis, retaining the Ringsted services on the other half hour, so a bit more variety again. Route learning had now become a whole new science as one had now to be booked with a Driving Instructor over the route involved, followed by the completion of a written form, plus a test on iPad; a far cry from when one just went and found a driver to ride with. There was still a steady flow of trainees to keep one on one's toes but spread out so that one could also have periods of driving alone as although I liked to impart my knowledge to new colleagues, it was also nice when they returned to school and one could be oneself again!

The next year, 2016, started off with an episode in February when on waiting to take over an MG set at København, I was approached by a 'test' driver from Aarhus depot, together with an Instructor from the help panel who was to have a practical day on the said class of train to enable him to be more competent when a driver was seeking assistance. I had had dealings with this Instructor before with the door problems in Valby in 2007, and I regarded him as a bit of an idiot. They wished to have my train to Kalundborg, a rush hour semi-fast working, to which I agreed, although I would remain in the cab as I still had overall responsibility. As far out as Holbæk, the ATC system is operative, which shows the allowed speed at all times, but after Holbæk one drives only after what the signals outside show. The Danish signalling system is speed control, which means that one has all relevant speeds written in the sectional appendices and all home signals show the allowed speed into the station, which has to be adhered to from the signal.

We left Holbæk and the next stop was Mørkøv, where we were booked to cross another train and, as expected, the home signal showed a speed of 60km/hr, the Instructor not showing any reaction, not even when I pointed out what the signal was showing, and he just replied that there was plenty of room, to which I said that if he did not respond now then he would not be taking my train any further. He braked the train down to the required speed but sulked during the

Class ME 1528, Kalundborg , first of class in new livery, 28/10/16

rest of the journey. These 'panel' Instructors were not all well liked and, as said before, a lot of time could be wasted with unnecessary discussions. For example, one evening, I relieved a class MG set and found that the rear cab door had a defective lock, and as the operating instructions stipulated that all cab doors not in use should be locked then I refused to take the train, to which I got the reply that I could use the guard to keep an eye on said door, until I pointed out that the guard had other duties, including giving me the signal to start, which he could not do from the rear cab. I parked the set and then travelled passenger to København to pick up my back working.

Twice in my career I had door problems with DD-stock where the Instructor's help was sadly lacking. The first was as stated before at Valby; the other incident was when relieving a train at København H to work to Østerport and then return to Kalundborg. The driver whom I relieved said that all was okay but when changing ends, I would probably experience a defective door warning, but that would be my problem and he promptly disappeared! On changing ends, I saw that there was a tail lamp switched on between two carriages, and after switching that off I made the new cab ready, and lo and behold, no door lamps blinking. This is because the ZWS system has to be able to 'find' the rear of the train to complete the door circuits, and this meant that when driving from the trailer carriage it found the tail lamp on the locomotive, thus no problems, but from the locomotive the carriage tail lamp was on, thus there was only control on half the train. I phoned the panel Instructor and made out that the problem was still there, to which he replied that I could continue as it had been there all day, and as long as the guard looked after the doors at each station then it was safe to continue! How many drivers had worked this train during the day? I then told him that I had resolved the problem, explaining what had happened and then saying that he would now be reported. This case went right up to the highest level in DSB's safety department. Reporting people was not something I made a habit of, three times in thirty years, as I always considered it best to resolve any problems directly with the person concerned, but those three occasions were of a much more serious nature.

On starting with DSB, all passenger stock, apart from inter-city units, was painted red, with the locomotives in red with black side panels and inter-city in white with red doors. In June 2000, two class ME (1509 and 1511) had a side-on collision at Kalundborg depot and were thus selected for an experimental new livery of all-over red, with DSB's new logo in blue depicted in large format. No further examples were so painted as when the DD-stock arrived in a grey and dark blue livery, it was decided that class ME would also be dark blue with large red logo, the reverse of 1509/1511. All multiple units were also repainted grey and blue. At first, it was only the ME locomotives modified with ZWS control that were repainted, but after the arrival of further DD carriages then the last sixteen would also be blue, but just with foil and not a full repaint. The remaining regional stock had also received blue foil but in the end looked terrible as the foil had difficulty adhering to the underlying rust patches! Then, in 2016, it was decided that red, in a shade very much like the current DB red, would be the colour of the future. One class MF dmu, 5051, received the new livery and then several class ME. I worked the first one, 1528, fresh from the paint shops on 28th October, my photo being taken at Værslev and myself taking a picture on arrival at Kalundborg.

The year 2017 seems to have been a year where nothing happened as I have only noted one day of any significance, when a level crossing was defective at Mørkøv. This meant getting verbal permission from the signalman to pass the starter signal at danger and proceed with caution to the defective crossing, where I had to activate the barriers from the local control box. Now, there are six sets of barriers between Mørkøv and Regstrup, the next crossing station, and having used so much time, all the others also showed defective on approach. This is because all the crossings are operated on a timer, and if the approach is slow as when running under caution (40km/hr) then the time runs out and the barriers rise, so each crossing has to be activated manually. This costs twenty minutes and can affect the timetable quite considerably, especially if the problem occurs inthe rush hour, when there can be several train crossings between Kalundborg and Holbæk.

So now we jump to 2018, when there are several incidents of note. This was also a year with some new recruits to the depot and therefore as Driver Instructors we were kept quite busy. The first incident was on 16th February whilst working the first morning departure with 2 x class MG. It was a frosty morning with a light covering of snow, when on rounding a curve we were met with the sight of about ten to twelve deer standing on the track. We were travelling at 120km/hr and I said to my trainee not to brake as we were too close to avoid a collision. All but two managed to jump away, and then there was an almighty bang and I saw a set of antlers fly by the windscreen as we continued to the next stop, where we could see what damage there was. I informed the signalman as to what had happened and after finding that the whole right-hand bottom corner of the train was cracked (glass fibre) and hanging rather loose, I then decided that we would continue to København with reduced speed. A cover to external el-supply was also missing, plus there was blood, hair, etc., etc., plastered down the side of the first carriage; not a pretty sight and not a very nice smell, either.

Only four days later, it was an ME that had problems, at first losing twenty minutes when it gave up the ghost with defects showing for ETH, electric brake, inverter and power surge. A walk of just under 200 metres back to the locomotive and I managed to revive it, and continuing the journey it ended with an arrival twelve minutes late. A defective gear on 2 x MG resulted in an eighteen-minute late start in the beginning of March, meaning that the path to Roskilde was lost, having to follow a stopping train to Holbæk with a twenty-five minute late arrival in Kalundborg as a result. On Sunday, 6th May there occurred a most strange episode. My trainee and I had booked on at 09.05 for a ten-hour duty and had covered most of the day, running first to Østerport and back to København H, with 2 x MG then with an ER set to Slagelse and return and should then just have returned to Kalundborg with an MG. We relieved the train on time and then all signals went to red, and a group of heavily armed police went into action clearing the platforms and emptying our train but completely ignoring us sitting in the cab. We never did find out what it was all about, but we sat there for three quarters of an hour before being allowed to continue and were not too pleased, as the day was long enough as it was.

The next thing of any note was on 28th August when booking on at 06.51, I was informed that my train was cancelled and that I was to take a taxi to København. I questioned the wisdom of that decision as it was the rush hour, to which I received the reply that there was plenty of time before my next working to Slagelse. The taxi arrived half an hour after booking on, and the journey took one hour and twenty-seven minutes, when for the last twenty minutes our supervisor kept ringing to find out where I was! On arrival, my train was still standing at the platform waiting for me! Only a small delay but one that could have been avoided by having taken the next train from Kalundborg! The next incident was just a week later when after having prepared 2 x MG, I shunted to the platform and changed ends where the screen showed only one set (!), the rear set apparently having disappeared. Informing the signalman of my dilemma, I went to the middle of the train to uncouple, which proved to be rather difficult, but I managed it in the end so that I could drive to København with just one set, but now control had decided to cancel the train and it ended up with me just taking the one set as ECS, leaving the other set at the platform.

Towards the end of the year, I experienced once again a car standing on the wrong side of the barriers in Jyderup station. I don't know what the problem is there as other colleagues have had the same experience, maybe a larger percentage of the local residents who should not be in possession of a driving licence. An extra responsibility for the Driving Instructors had now been introduced, which involved taking two drivers out of their roster to give them a traction brush-up. As there was normally no stock berthed in Kalundborg during the day at that time, we had to travel to København to find suitable material, which also made the day's instruction rather concentrated. My first try at this was with two colleagues for a brush-up with ME + DD stock, which went off rather well within the time allotted and, in fact, that was the only time that I was involved with that form of instruction as we were six Driving Instructors at the depot to share out the work, and time was now running out for me as I had decided to retire during the next year.

Class MG 5865 ready for opening of new station Kalundborg Øst 8/12/2018

The last thing of any note in 2018 was also rather special. On the outskirts of Kalundborg there is situated a large medicine factory owned by Novo Nordisk, specialising in the production of insulin and having many employees. It had been decided to construct a halt right by the factory to try and attract more people to use the train to ease traffic congestion on the local roads. This halt was to be officially opened on 8th December, and Tommy asked me if I would like to drive the opening train, to which I agreed. We were to use 2 x MG sets, which we decorated with flags at both ends, then working from Kalundborg to KalundborgØst, which was open to the public free of charge. I then worked the train ECS to Værslev to wait in the passing loop until required to return, the whole duty taking about six hours.

So now we enter 2019, my last year with DSB. The year did not start off very well, with a tragic accident on the bridge over the Storebælt (the Great Belt) when a truck semi-trailer became loose on a DB Cargo freight and swung out into the path of an inter-city train comprising 2 x MG sets, tearing the side out of the first part of the train, killing eight passengers and injuring several more. Incredibly, the driver received only light injuries.

As for my own work, I had decided to retire at the close of September, based on various criteria. My birthday is in March but my seniority date was 1st June, giving me thirty years' civil servant pension, and then if I continued to September I would also be eligible to go straight to my state pension as well, so that is what I decided to do. Tommy was not too happy to receive my resignation but that's life! There had been agreement between the union and DSB that train drivers if working until the age of sixty-five had not reached the maximum thirty-seven years for a full civil servant pension then they would receive up to a maximum of five years on top of what they had earned. That agreement had for a time been revoked by DSB along with a lot of other agreements but had recently been reinstated, so I ended up with thirty-five years, which was nearly a full pension.

Class MF 5251, Kalundborg 17/05/2019

The last few months seemed to pass rather quickly, with just a few incidents. One day on returning from Slagelse with an ER set, I got an error on the ATC system that invoked an emergency braking. There was nothing one could do until coming to a standstill, and having done so, I could then reset and release the brake, whereupon I then had to receive permission from the signalman to resume the journey after giving information about what had happened. The only problem now was that the train had come to a standstill in the middle of a neutral section (!) but luckily, after releasing the brake, the train began to roll gently in the right direction and I was able to get 25Kv again.

We had at this time some trouble with duties being altered for no apparent reason other than to create frustration and delays. One morning, my duty had been altered to book on fifty minutes later than normal, as if it was a dmu set rostered and covering up the fact that there was nobody to help with brake testing. The stock rostered was in fact ME + DD and having to carry out the brake test alone, the result was a twenty-nine minute late start. This occurred several times without any noticeable consequences as duty alterations continued to be full of errors. A second incidence of the rolling capabilities of a failed train happened nearly at the end of my career. I had arrived at Valby, where the ME locomotive at the rear of the train suffered an engine stop on the way into the platform. I went back to investigate and could see a jet of coolant spraying out onto the platform and could thus conclude that it was a failure. The guard emptied the train for passengers and I then arranged with the signalman that I would see if the train could roll towards København and that I would be signalled into track 26, which is a terminal platform and the nearest to me. At first, on releasing the brake, nothing happened, but then it began to move and actually reached 2530 km/hr, which was perfect for the approach to track 26. As I came to a standstill, the brakes were fully applied as the level of air in the system had reached a critical level and the (roughly translated) driving lock operated, a safety component designed to prevent the train from moving before the required air pressure is reached. The delay incurred with this failure amounted to twenty minutes, far less than if an assisting train had been summoned.

It was now clear that my last day driving would be 30th August as the whole of September would be used for remaining holiday and lieu days, and even in August there were only sixteen working days left, including two failures! One was a defective start motor with ME1523, and the second was three days before finishing when preparing 2 x MG and the computer would not allow an automatic brake test.

So now came the last day of my career. Normally, one was taken off the rostered duty and together with one's group leader, one would travel out to Holbæk, for example, and then drive back to the depot, but I had decided that I would work my own duty so that I could also say farewell to anybody I met in København. Therefore, I booked on at 04.54, preparing 2 x MG (5601/5676) and working a rushhour train to the capital. The roster clerk had removed the middle part of the duty so that I had plenty of time for myself. Tommy would accompany me on the return trip together with my son, daughter-in-law and their baby, for whom he had arranged cab passes, plus an Instructor from the training school, so the cab was pretty much filled up. To mark that it was my last day, I had shunned the normal uniform and dressed in a dust coat and my original cap, which caused a few comments along the way. A handful of colleagues from København also joined the train, which comprised a single class MG (5623), and at 10.43 I departed København H for the last time as a train driver, and for once there were no delays en route. Tommy had put up a couple of flags in the windscreen and there were many colleagues giving a final wave as they passed. Whilst waiting for the right away at Jyderup, I was called up by the signalwoman to wish me well in my retirement and then a warning that there had been a report of somebody trespassing on the track near Svebølle station and that I should proceed with caution. On nearing Svebølle, I could see that the train I was due to cross with had arrived and that there was draped a huge flag across the track in front of it and that there were several passengers and staff waving as I entered the platform. It was my good Driving Instructor colleague, Jimmi, who had charge of the train and had arranged the little happening.

It was the last stretch into Kalundborg (with a right-time arrival at 12.10), where on passing the depot there was gathered a large group of colleagues, and at the platform my wife, daughters, grandchildren, friends and more colleagues were waiting to greet me. It was all a bit overwhelming but in a nice way. The platform monitor was set up to say that it was my last train before retiring, and my relief had booked on earlier to relieve me on arrival instead of in the yard. When the train was empty of passengers then all my well-wishers boarded and we were transported out to the depot where my retirement reception was to be held, organised by Tommy and paid for by DSB. The weather was perfect, a warm sunny summer's day, so we could be outside. There was a hot sausage stand, cakes, snacks and soft drinks (as it was on railway property), and there were around seventy to eighty guests who had turned up from far and wide. Tommy made a speech as did two of my colleagues, Maiken and Steen, and myself. A table had been set up in the depot on which was loaded very many gifts, quite a few of which had an alcoholic content! After a couple of hours, we adjourned to the neighbouring bowling centre for an intake of something a little stronger to drink.

So that was that, the end of a forty-eight-year working life, the bulk of which (forty-one years) was as a railway employee. I had still one month's employment left but that was at home, with just a single visit to the depot to hand in keys, iPad, mobile phone, etc., and then free from having to get up at some godforsaken time in all types of weather to go to work. Have not missed it at all!

Driver's desk, class ME 26/08/2019

Kalundborg home signal with speed restriction 40km, 26/08/19

Brake slip as always used on loco-hauled trains 26/08/2019

My last class ME trip, 26/8/2019

Last working day, 30/8/2019, myself with group leader Tommy Jørgensen at København

Taking over class MG 5623 for final trip to Kalundborg, 30/8/2019

Last arrival at Kalundborg, with message from Roskilde signallingcentre 30/08/2019

Farewell speech, Kalundborg depot, 30/8/2019

Reflections

I consider myself lucky to have had the opportunity to have two careers within the railway industry, which have been just as much a hobby as a job. The job of train driver especially has, at least until more recent times, been a job with a lot of freedom where you just got on with the job without much outside interference and were trained to take snap decisions and to stand by them even if the result turned out to be the wrong one. The motive power department has always been like a close-knit family and a race apart from the rest of the industry, this being the same both in the UK and in Denmark, and although there have been attempts to congregate rather than segregate the different grades, there have been only partial successes as drivers tend to keep together with other drivers and guards with guards as generally it boils down to the fact that there are clashes of personality types. I think that this starts already on the first day of employment when some forms of tradition are handed down, and of course the nature of the job driving trains, sitting alone for most of the time, instills a greater sense of independence, negating the need to be together with other grades with whom youdo not have so much in common. I could also see this when employed as a shunter/yard foreman as we kept together and closed ranks against others even though we were working together with drivers, this being especially so at the larger depots.

It has been a most interesting process working for two state railway organisations that really were not so different from each other. Both had been originally built up under a type of military hierarchy, the main difference being that in Denmark one could be on firstname terms even with top management, unheard of in England, where higher management were referred to as officers! It has of course not always been so in Denmark but something that has evolved over the years throughout Danish society.

As stated earlier, I chose to apply for a driver'sjob at a multiple unit depot out of necessity, not preference, as of course locomotive work is much more interesting, though a lot noisier! On reaching the position of driver with DSB and being stationed at Kalundborg, the work was nearly all with locomotives, with just two weekday duties when half of the work was with dmus, the percentage increasing with the years until we learnt the class MG, and then the balance was distinctly in favour of multiple units. However, class MG, in my opinion,was one of the best trains that we had. Granted, there had been many problems with their introduction, but by the time we received them reliability was beginning to improve, and we learnt a lot of tricks to get us out of trouble as driving them so often we gained a lot of experience. They also had a spacious and well-laidout cab and being fairly heavy were very stable at all speeds, so all in all a good workplace.

The type of person employed as a train driver is also very similar in the two countries, with the same approach to the job, same type of humour, etc. There has, however, been a change in recent years in Denmark as in earlier times one had to have completed an apprenticeship as a metal worker, mechanic, etc., to be considered for the job, but now one can enter the industry straight from high school as opposed to having any job experience, with the same happening in the UK after the abolition of the grade of secondman, which was a form of apprenticeship. For Driving Instructors, this has meant that some instruction as to how one should react to the various challenges arising from roster clerks, control, etc., has also been necessary. That is my point of view, not necessarily shared by all Instructors, but I like to think that I have sent my trainees on the right path and encouraged them not to accept everything at face value.

Since I retired, there has been a bit of a clear-out at Kalundborg depot of the older generation, and we are five that have established a small club where we meet several times a year, when we can partake of food and drink and talk over the good and not so good times that we had on the railway. All five of us have been active in the union, so we have a lot in common. I am still a member of the Dansk Jernbane-forbund and keep *à jour* with what is happening within the industry. Working for the railway has been one long process of learning which you never finish as there is always something new to absorb, and as the years pass, it does not get easier to adjust to new methods of learning, for example, via computer instead of classroom, and I am personally glad that I got out before becoming involved in the new signalling system, ERTMS. Would I do it again? Most definitely as driving trains is one of the best jobs going, if one can agree with the working hours! That sounds a bit of a contradiction with the previous paragraph, but if one enters the industry today then the older methods of working are not totally engrained. It does however crave stability on the home front as one's free time can be quite restricted, and after so many years of working every second weekend and many bank holidays, plus the unsocial hours, it is quite liberating to start a new life as a pensioner. I have been very lucky to have an understanding wife to support me and our family when once again having to juggle dates for various family arrangements and having to put up with all the awkward shifts.

Glossary

UK:

E4/C2X – classes of 'Brighton' steam locomotives
Q– a Southern Railway steam locomotive
EMU – electric multiple unit
DEMU – diesel electric multiple unit
DMMU – diesel mechanical multiple unit
4COR/2BIL/2HAL – pre-war built Emus.
4SUB – post-war (1948) suburban EMU
EPB/CEP/BEP – 1951/7 EMUs
CIG/BIG/VEP – 1963 EMUs
MLV – Motor luggage van (electric/battery-powered)
ECS – Empty coaching stock
ETH – Electric train heating
Class 73 – Electro-diesel locomotive
Class 33/47 – Diesel-electric locomotives
Class 08/09 – Diesel-electric shunting locomotives

DENMARK:

Class ME/MZ – Diesel-electric locomotives with General Motors engines
Class MR – Diesel-hydraulic DMU based on a German design (Class 628)
Class MF/MG – Diesel-mechanical (automatic gear) DMUs
Class ER – Electric mu
DD – Double-deck carriages
DSB – Danish State Railways
København – Copenhagen

www.ingramcontent.com/pod-product-compliance
Lightning Source LLC
Chambersburg PA
CBHW070457090426

42735CB00012B/2584